A ROMANCE

OF

BIDSTON HILL:

OR,

LOVE AND FORTUNE.

BY F. A.

"A love so violent, so strong, so sure,
That neither age can change, nor art can cure."

COPYRIGHT

LIVERPOOL:
JAMES WOOLLARD, 54, CASTLE STREET.

CHAPTER I.

THE winter during which some of the events depicted in our story occurred was remarkable in many respects, and one never to be forgotten in at least one home in, what we shall name, the dear old town of Crompton. Never had the oldest inhabitant in that charming retreat remembered a winter in which the cold was so intense, the snow and ice so plentiful, sorrows so absent, and the prospect of a Merry Christmas so certain. There had seemed, thus far, to be no limit to love, pleasure, and success; at least so thought May Jeffries, in the first joy of her early love, as she glided lightly on through the forest, the tall trees of which, in summer, cast their soft pleasant shade over the happy home of her childhood. Crompton was at all times a desirable locality, sheltered on every side from the cold winds and with everything accessible which makes life so charming and enjoyable. In spring time, when the flowers were tinting the undergrowth with their varied hues, and the birds were sprinkling the fragrant air with their music, everything seemed to impress one's mind with the idea of perfect beauty; and the same charm seemed to exert its influence right on through the successive seasons. Even in winter, when the forest trees were enveloped in feathery snow and the icy hand of the Old King was visible on all sides, the feeling was not absent, but left its trace upon the mind sensible to Nature's loveliness. And now, as May hurried on towards her home, with nimble foot and happy glance, it was no difficult matter to conjecture that the thoughts which were passing in her heart, and so plainly discernible in her countenance, were in harmony with the surrounding scene.

May was a handsome brunette of eighteen. Her features were clearly and finely cut, her dark brown eyes sparkled like diamonds beneath their well arched brows, whilst her mouth betrayed a strange mingling of determination and gentleness in her character. When animated by bright and happy thoughts, as now, her loveliness was irresistible, and even when her features reposed, there was something so queenly about her, that one's admiration was involuntarily aroused.

And think you that her gracefulness, her amiability, her vivacity, were lost upon those who were fortunate enough to class her amongst their acquaintances?

Frank Atherton, had you seen him a few hours later on this day, in the act of perusing a neatly-written letter, and enquired the cause of his exultant joy, would immediately have dispelled any lingering doubts on the subject.

Frank was the son of a well-to-do tradesman residing in Liverpool, and, to judge from the testimony of his friends, was an exceedingly fine young fellow, who was not only much admired for his steadiness of purpose, but also for his kindly and generous disposition. It was not often that Frank had the opportunity of seeing May, and hitherto business matters, and an occasional visit to a relative residing in the neighbourhood, had alone brought him near to that one who now appeared to compass all that was necessary to complete his happiness.

Her vision ever haunted him; her accomplishments, her charms, were his unending theme. Often he would appear sad and dejected, like the man who feels that his hopes are but vain shadows, ever enticing him by their presence, and yet ever eluding his grasp. In short, Frank felt that he loved May deeply, loved her with all the affection of which his large heart was capable, but yet he doubted whether she who allured him would ever consent to be the dear companion of his life.

Admittedly there are many anxieties which cast their shadows over life's pathway, but to a man who has been caught in the meshes of love there is perhaps none so painful as that which is provoked by circumstances adversive to his suit.

Frank had been conscious of the existence of the tender passion in his heart for some three months past, and had, in consequence of his imagining that his suit would prove an unsuccessful one, been at times the victim of sad and harassing thoughts. He had met May under circumstances scarcely favourable to the attainment of his object, and had been seen by her in the performance of acts which, in the absence of explanation, were not calculated to impress her favourably in, his behalf. Not being on very intimate terms, an explanation would have amounted to a confession, and he had thus to bear all that irritability of which thought is ever productive when actions, philanthropic and excellent in their motive, are misconstrued into sinful and disreputable practices.

A friend of Frank's had unfortunately become mixed up in an affair of rather questionable character, and had fallen into ways of vice which seemed for a time to have obtained the complete mastership over him; and in his efforts to extricate his friend from vile associates and habits, Frank had had duties of a not very desirable nature to perform, and which, though prompted by Christian motives, were liable to misinterpretation.

It was in the performance of one of these actions that May had seen him on the occasion of her last visit to Liverpool, and her heart had been filled with anxious foreboding, lest the man, whom she secretly admired, might after all be but an associate of men unworthy of the name, and necessarily as bad as they.

But this impression was happily removed. On her return journey she encountered an old friend who was well acquainted with Frank, and knew all about the mission of mercy upon which he was engaged; and as the conversation turned upon May's favourite topic, the cause of Frank's peculiar conduct was so satisfactorily explained, nay so enthusiastically praised, that May felt her estimation of him very much increased.

Thus it happened that the act which Frank concluded had destroyed his every chance of winning May had really raised him to a place in her heart he had never previously occupied, proving once again the truth of the old saying, that "a good deed carries with it its own reward."

Early in Christmas week Frank had visited May's home, and after transacting an important matter of business with Squire Jeffries, he had been invited to spend the evening with the family.

The Squire was a kind, genial soul, whose chief delight consisted in his endeavours to render everybody with whom he came into contact as happy as possible. He often remarked, as he rubbed his hands together with evident satisfaction, that he saw no good in cultivating gloomy, sad, desponding feelings, because he felt that there was ever some creature in the world in a much worse plight than he was, and therefore he had every reason for thankfulness. "Get," he would say, bringing his hand down upon his knee, to give emphasis to his statements, "the love of God in your heart, keep on the sunny side of life, look at everything in its brightest and best light, imagine no evil of anybody unless you have positive proof, try to produce a reflex of the sunshine which warms and gladdens your own heart on the hearts of those around you, and then, I assert, you have found the key to that true happiness after which men are ever seeking."

Frank never remembered spending a more enjoyable evening—the Squire, with his pleasant kind manner—May so graceful and so pleasing—all tended to raise his

hopes and to dash to the earth the bitter cup of
despair which had already been half raised to his lips.
Never had the time glided so rapidly, never had man
experienced such emotions of pleasure, as Frank on this
memorable evening. He drank in her every word as if
he had been imbibing the nectar of life; whilst the
admiration he felt for her was clearly visible in his
handsome face. This did not pass unperceived by May,
for the eye of love sees quickly, and her heart leaped
joyously, as she felt that Frank admired and loved her.
No word indicative of his feelings had escaped him, and
indeed he did not yet feel capable of uttering any.
The conversation, at first, was rather uninteresting, the
young people feeling that "awkwardness" which generally affects the amorous in the early stages of their
courtship, but which has yet the redeeming feature that
it affords to those concerned a glimpse of the cause,
and thus tends eventually to draw them into closer
communion.

As the evening glided on, however, they became more
at their ease, and the topics of their conversation changed
from vague generalities to personal tastes and aspirations.
Being well versed in classical music, and able to speak
of and contrast the merits of the various celebrated
composers, May soon made a captive of our hero, who

was also an enthusiast, and when she illustrated her
remarks instrumentally, he could readily have imagined
himself in fairyland. From music the conversation
naturally turned to poetry; and May, who dearly loved
argument, startled Frank, by asserting that, to her mind,
poetry was superior to music. For some time an
animated discussion was kept up, but this, however,
finally ended by their concluding that the one was
rendered more enjoyable and agreeable by the existence
of the other. Various other subjects followed, to the
enjoyment of both, until the Squire reminded them that
the time for Frank's departure was at hand.

"Good bye, Miss Jeffries," said Frank, tendering his
hand to her, "I trust soon again to have the pleasure
of meeting you, and of spending an hour in your
company."

"I trust so too," said May, smiling, and returning
the pressure of his hand with a warmth which made his
heart thrill with almost uncontrollable emotion; "good
bye," and waving her handkerchief she disappeared from
view; the door closed, and Frank stood upon the
pavement, like one awakening from a dream, the locality
of which had been heaven, to find himself upon the
earth again. Frank was not long, however, in recovering
himself, and soon he was travelling on by the night train

And the moon shone brightly, lighting up the forest, and filling it with weird and fantastic forms, and its soft, silvery light seemed to whisper "peace" to Frank's troubled heart, "all will be well; May shall be yours, and your future shall be all that you anticipate and desire."

Little did he imagine the sad and painful events which must take place before he would again see that dear face which had smiled upon him so lovingly as he took his departure, and which seemed, even now, to be looking down upon him with its gentle, sweet, encouraging glance.

A few days before the Christmas festival, Frank's heart was cheered by the receipt of the invitation to spend the season at Crompton, which May had just posted when we first made her acquaintance, and in which she had, with a woman's instinct, emphasised the fact that *she* would be extremely happy to see him.

Frank hastily perused the letter, and without delay forwarded his acceptance.

Having despatched the note to the post, Frank set out, intending to spend the evening at Bidston, where he considered he would feel free to meditate upon the bliss which he felt would soon be his. As he left his home he did not notice that three men, who had for some time been watching for his exit, quitted the passage in which they had been lurking, and followed closely behind him.

They were powerful but disreputable looking men, and from their demeanour it was evident that their intentions were none of the best.

CHAPTER II.

ABOUT half a mile from Squire Jeffries' residence there stood, facing the main road, and in the centre of a handsome garden, an exceedingly well-built mansion, which was occupied at this time by a Mr. Robert Dove and his family. He had been very successful as a Cotton Merchant at Manchester, and had in a few years amassed a considerable fortune. Thinking that his health would be benefited by residing more in the country, he had purchased the "Roseville" Estate, and had continued to live there for the greater portion of each year.

He was assisted in his business by his son Charles, a tall, thin, excitable young fellow of about twenty-eight summers.

Often a dark, sinister expression might be seen to pass over this young man's countenance, and his lips to tremble with inward and ill-controlled anger. Often, when alone, he would mutter audibly, "He must be removed, or all is lost."

The father and son had many long and private conversations together, and on 'Change it had been noticed that they appeared much out of humour. Ugly whispers were soon rife, all pointing to the fact of a speedy failure of the firm.

Whether this was so or not, it was certainly evident that something of more than ordinary importance was about to, or had really occurred; and also that that something was not of a gladdening and desirable nature.

This state of affairs had continued for some two or three months before Christmas; and as each month disappeared it might be noticed that the Doves became more irritable and excited, that their secret consultations were more numerous, and that a frown, dark and portentous, was scarcely ever absent from the features of either father or son.

The morning of the day on which Frank had passed his pleasant and never-to-be-forgotten evening with May, the Doves had a lengthy and serious conversation in their city office.

"Charles! Charles!" said Mr. Dove, "we must do something immediately to avert this catastrophe. It

will never do that the hitherto honoured and esteemed
name of Dove should now be sullied by a failure.
Would that I had never meddled with that last lot of
cotton. It was rash, very rash—I ought to have known
better. The market had reached its highest point when
I speculated, and then came the drop, the dreadful
drop, which threatens to bring ruin upon me and my
family. I have tried every means to prevent this
calamity which stares me in the face, but without avail,
and there now appears to me to be but one means
of escape—but one way by which we can be saved
from poverty. Poverty, did I say? Death it should have
been, for the very name, not to speak of the reality,
sends a thrill of anguish through my heart, which
threatens to stop its beating. I have tasted the power,
the enjoyment of wealth, revelled in all the advantages
which it can procure, and now to be despoiled of my
riches, to become a beggar—it is more than I can bear."

"But, father, all is not yet lost!" said Charles.
"The means of escape to which you referred may yet
be secured!" "Secured!" responded Mr. Dove,—"what
success have you had hitherto? I had built my hopes
upon you, and now the building has been shattered,
and despair hangs over me like a dense cloud. The
riches which I toiled for unceasingly to be taken from

me in one fell sweep—the blow is too heavy—I cannot but succumb—I must die—die!!" And with an expression of bitter anguish he turned from his son, and paced moodily up and down, up and down the office, with his head bent upon his chest, and his eyes fixedly regarding the floor. Surely he had aged at least twenty years within the last few weeks; the utter want of comfort, heavenly comfort, had left his heart a prey to all the terrors which are born of chagrin, remorse, and ruin. He had laid up treasures upon earth, he had built his house upon the sand, and the wind and the waves of adversity were coming to destroy his property, and with it his only source of joy and comfort.

How happy they who can say their treasure is in heaven, their house upon the rock, secure from the wind and waves of time, and ever standing like a beacon upon some rocky coast, shedding a gleam of guiding, gladdening, comforting light over the dangers which surround it.

"Do not speak thus, father," said Charles, "you torment me to desperation. You know I have done my best to secure the prize which was to bring sufficient wealth to our family to divert this threatening danger, and yet you cast these reproaches in my teeth. You know how the obstacle which prevents my grasping the coveted object can best be removed; say but the word, and the means will be put into execution."

"And do you really think I have sunk so low, that I can descend to the commission of the crime which you meditate," said Mr. Dove, glaring angrily at his son.

"That is the only outlet I can see, and we must either use it or be reduced to beggary," responded Charles. "The scheme I have propounded to you is not so vile in its nature that you—you who have not hesitated at the performance of many doubtful acts in connection with your business—need have any qualms of conscience about it. We need not be known in the matter. Jerry Mills assured me that for a hundred pounds he would arrange the whole affair, and see it carried out in its entirety. He has some associates to whom he will entrust the commission, and he alone will be known as the principal. I see no grounds for either your fears or qualms of conscience."

"Well, well, I am doubtful," said Mr. Dove, "as to the result. Even if Jerry succeeded, you may not, and then the money, which we can ill afford, will have been thrown to the winds."

"But I am certain to succeed," rejoined Charles.

"Are you," replied his father ironically, "you must be certain of nothing in this life, except it be death."

"Well, then," said Charles, turning upon his heel with the intention of quitting the room, "you must accept the inevitable."

"Stay, stay, do not be so hasty; give me time to think the matter over," said Mr. Dove, pettishly. "The crisis must be averted at all hazards." And then, with a little more of sociability in his manner, he added—"Be seated, Charles, and tell me again briefly how you propose to cope with our present difficulty."

Charles seated himself in close proximity to his father, and was about to proceed in a low tone with the explanation of his plan, when a loud knock was heard at the door of the counting-house.

The door was opened by one of the clerks, and then a coarse voice was heard, roughly demanding to see Mr. Charles Dove. "He is engaged at present, and likely to be so for some time," replied the clerk. "Is it anything that I can attend to?" "No," curtly replied the stranger. "I want and must see Mr. Dove hisself, and at once!!" "Very well, then, I will announce you; what name shall I say?" "Jerry Mills," answered the man.

Charles, on hearing this, immediately sprang to his feet and rang the bell for the clerk, who, on making his appearance, was ordered to usher in Mr. Mills.

Jerry Mills was anything but a prepossessing individual. He was a coarse, brutal looking man, of moderate height, and of a build more suggestive of feats of strength than of elegance.

As he entered the private office he glanced quickly around, and then perceiving that Mr. Dove, junior, was not the only other person present, he bowed slightly, and stood near the door fumbling with his hat, and looking at Charles askantly. From his manner it was apparent that he had something to impart to the latter which was not intended for the ears of a third party.

Charles was the first to break the silence. Approaching Jerry, he said, "good morning," at the same time extending his hand to him. "I suppose you have some important information for me? This is my father," he added, noticing Jerry's suspicious look, "so you need have no fear of disclosing your secret. Strange, we were just discussing the matter, and as you have now put in an appearance, I will ask you to explain your plan personally. Doubtless you have some fresh ideas or schemes to place before us which, if carried out, will render our success a certainty."

"I have," replied Jerry, after first turning the key in the door and glancing cautiously around, but——"But what?" said Charles, impatiently. "I s'pose there's no fear o' listeners?" "Not the slightest; we are perfectly secure here, you may proceed without reserve," replied Charles, somewhat curtly, being annoyed at the delay.

"Well," said Jerry, still speaking very slowly, "the money will be all right, will it?" "Certainly, certainly," rejoined Charles. "Well, then, I've got two pals as is ready to give me a hand with the job, and we've made all prep'ritions—just say the word, and we'll get to bisness at once." "Yes, yes; but how do you propose to proceed?" enquired Mr. Dove. "O, you may leave that to me, there's no fear o' such wary birds as Jerry Mills an' his pals being nabbed!"

"But will you not give us some idea as to the plan of action you have decided upon?" said Dove, senior, "we would like to hear something definite from you!"

"Well," said Jerry, musingly, "perhaps I might"— and then drawing his chair quite close to the desk at which the Doves sat, he whispered hoarsely—"We'll try to get him to the river side, watch our chance, tap his skull, and throw his corpus into the bay. Ye'r see that there smack I've on the Mersey is a tidy sized craft, with room to hide several such as him aboard, an' when we've got him safe, we'll drop down with the ebb to the bay, where we'll sink him in deep water."

As Jerry said this, both the Doves started and looked at one another horror-stricken at the nature of the crime, and the coolness with which Jerry explained it. They had thought that if the man who stood between them and their booty were removed for a year or two from England, it would have been sufficient for their purpose, and as they were not to be known as parties to such removal, they considered they would be perfectly safe.

"But, Jerry," said Charles, "when we last conferred together, you told me you thought you could arrange for his being carried to some lonely island in the South Sea, where, at least, he could be kept in security for a year or two."

"Yes," said Jerry, "I did, but the Cap'n o' the 'Lively Lass' is agen it; he is afeared o' a deskivery, an' I knows o' no other Cap'n fit for the job. You had better leave a cove to settle the affair in his own quiet way, you needn't know how it's done. The man is shifted, that's good enough for you."

"We are not parties to murder," said Dove, senior, "you must understand that clearly. If you take that step, it will be entirely at your own risk. We wash our hands of all responsibility in the matter."

"Quite agreeable, guv'nor; 'spose yee'll give a cove some chink to be going on with?" responded Jerry, a

"Here are ten pounds, but mind no murder," said Mr. Dove, handing Jerry the money. "All right, guv'nor, then we'll get to work immegetly—good day and luck." Saying this, Jerry shuffled out of the room, hurried down the stairs leading from the office to the street, and rejoined his comrades, who were awaiting his return.

"Well, what luck?" said the tallest of the two burly ruffians. "We've got the Mister Doves in our power," responded Jerry, with a knowing wink, "and if this little job's done neatly, those swell coves will have to pay the piper to Jerry and his pals. No more work then, boys, we'll live on the perceeds o' this business."

So it is ever! Those who descend to the commission of vile and sinful deeds must not imagine that the success which attends their inhuman and immoral actions will carry with it immunity from pain and punishment. It is written—"The face of the Lord is against them that do evil, to cut off the remembrance of them from the earth. Evil shall slay the wicked, and they that hate the righteous shall be desolate." If the Doves imagined that they were to escape the evil consequences of their crime, they deceived themselves. Clouds, big with sorrow, anguish, and remorse, already began to darken the horizon of their future; and soon—oh, how soon—those clouds would break and scatter their contents relentlessly over the lives of those two men, who in vain might seek to shelter themselves from the terrible downpouring.

The trio proceeded to the Victoria Railway Station, and in a short time were being carried swiftly by the express train to Liverpool. Being alone in the compartment which they had entered, they discussed, in low tones, their plan of action, and decided upon the course they would adopt on their arrival.

It was arranged that they should first make their way to Jerry's smack, the "Saucy Poll," which lay moored behind the Landing Stage, and then, after making all needful preparations, remove her to a convenient position for their purpose, in the river. Here they would moor her, and wait for a favourable opportunity of getting the one who was to become a sacrifice to their avarice on board. The smack was to be left in charge of young Mills (who was also in the plot), whilst the three men watched on shore for their prey.

On arriving at Lime Street Station, they at once set out for the Landing Stage; and by nine o'clock the same evening, the "Saucy Poll" lay moored just off New Brighton, and the three men were imbibing whisky toddy in the back parlour of the Crown and Anchor Inn, at the place last mentioned.

It was too late for them to do anything further that
night in connection with their brutal undertaking, and
they had, therefore, determined to spend what remained
of the evening in a manner as congenial to their tastes
as possible. The following day they would see what
progress could be made. They would first watch the
house in which their man was located, and on his
issuing forth would follow him, in the hope of an
opportunity presenting itself which would enable them
to carry out their designs successfully.

If such an opportunity did not arise, they would get
young Mills, who had received a fair education in
orthography, and a good one in villany, to write a note
for them, inviting the unsuspecting object of their
schemes to meet, at a late hour, some fictitious personage on the Cheshire side of the Mersey, under the
cloak of either business or benevolence.

Full of their plans, and labouring under the influence
of the strong spirits they were drinking, they chuckled
in anticipation of that success which they now felt would
certainly be theirs.

"No work, plenty o' cash and wittles, and all sorts
o' amoosements," said Jerry, laughing loudly, and shaking
hands for the seventh or eighth time with his companions.

And they congratulated one another, and pledged themselves again and again to be true to their vow of secrecy, and revelled in the scenes which their excited imaginations pictured would render bright and happy the remainder of their days.

We shall see whether all they picture and anticipate is realized—whether the cunning craft and might of the wicked, or the innocence and right of the just, succeed!

CHAPTER III.

IN order that you, my reader, may understand the preceding chapter, it will be necessary that you should accompany me to that picturesque little villa which adorns the entrance to High Street, in Crompton, and which rouses the envy of every passing connoisseur. It is built after the model of a Swiss châlet, and everything in connection with it, and its surrounding garden, indicate that the possessor is no ordinary personage, and one with ample means for gratifying luxurious and, perhaps, somewhat eccentric tastes.

An entrance into the interior will confirm abundantly all that is suggested by the exterior. The walls are hung with the peculiar description of tapestry which one finds in the interior of châlets on the French coast, at Fécamp and Étretat for instance, and old French furniture, and articles of vertû beautify the various

rooms. Everywhere, however, there is an indescribable
something which conveys to the mind the conviction
that the occupier of the villa is eccentric in habit, and
this conviction is in nowise weakened by an introduction
to the personage who is the owner of all these objects
of art and interest.

Eccentric people are generally a burden, and a source
of annoyance to those of their neighbours who have to
submit to the vagaries of their eccentricities, but to this
rule Mrs. Walton formed an exception. Her peculiar
manners had, however, quite ostracised her, and in
the whole town there were scarcely any who could
speak in kind, or other terms, of her, and still less
who could claim her as a friend. She had lived
in the neighbourhood for many years, and had come,
no one, with the exception of a relative who resided
some short distance from her, knew whence.

It was said by the gossips of the town that her
husband had been a wealthy and distinguished man,
but had died abroad, unfortunately, a few months after
his marriage.

This sad event, it was thought, had given rise to
her eccentricity of manner. For months at times she
would not see anybody, and would confine herself to
her rooms, and her books, having intercourse only with

an old and faithful domestic, who had either too much respect for her mistress, or was too wise and discreet to reveal the affairs of the household.

At other times she would allow one or two of her relatives to visit her, and would receive them with all cordiality, allowing the veil which usually hid from view her really kind and sympathetic disposition to be removed, and her fine and genuine character to make a full display of all its multifarious traits. This was especially so when her young nephew, Frank Atherton, paid her a visit.

She seemed to take a lively interest in everything which excited his attention, and would draw upon the resources of experience, the great privilege of the aged, for Frank's benefit and guidance.

Though well advanced in years, she had not forgotten, like so many aged people, it is to be regretted do, that once she had been young like Frank, and she could therefore the more readily enter into the subjects of his occupations and amusements of the present, as well as his plans and aspirations respecting the future.

It had been her custom for years to distribute, secretly, over an area of many miles, money and other comforts to the poor. How she discovered their wants, was known only to Betsy, her faithful adherent. Still her gifts were always well timed, and gave rise often to some little discussion amongst those benefited as to what the name of their benefactor might be.

These discussions, however, soon ceased, like all those which relate to benefits received. Alas, that men ever forget the good done to them, and allow their memories to retain the feelings which have been born of bad and spiteful words and actions! Were it the reverse of this, how much more friendly would this world be; "forgive and forget," would then not only be each man's motto, but be the living principle which would imbue the heart and life with a joy and sweetness hitherto unknown.

Mrs. Walton often cherished hopes of enlarging her sphere of usefulness, but these hopes were doomed to disappointment. One morning, when attending to her garden, she was seized with paralysis, and had to be carried to her room, there to await that summons which none can evade, and which comes often—aye very often —without the slightest warning of its approach.

A Doctor was immediately sent for, who, on examination, pronounced the case to be a very serious one. He said that the shock to the system was one which it was clearly evident Mrs. Walton could not long survive. She might linger for a year or two, but even this was very doubtful. In any case, she would never again be able to rise from her couch.

The only relative, within easy distance, was her cousin, Mr. Robert Dove, to whom we have already alluded, who, although not on the best terms with Mrs. Walton, owing to the cold reception that lady gave to the advances of his son, on hearing the news, at once hurried to her bed-side, in the hope that he could render some service which would prove acceptable to and place him on more amicable terms with her. As he passed down the steps leading to his home, he accosted his son Charles, whom he apprized in a few words of what had happened, and desired to consider in what way he could best instal himself into the affection of Mrs. Walton.

For some time past Mr. Dove and his son had plotted how to obtain the favour of their aged relative, in the hope that she would bequeath the whole, or, at least, the greater portion of her wealth to Charles, but so far they had not made much advance in the desired direction. They found that the affection and confidence they sought to obtain was given to another, and that their advances were received with a coldness of manner which led them almost to the conclusion that Mrs. Walton had discerned their secret designs.

True it is, that services rendered out of pure love and respect, and services given merely for the purpose of reward, are as gold compared to dross, and are, generally speaking, easily recognized. There is a cringing servility, an over-anxious desire to please, connected with the latter, which the former lacks, and which, therefore, all the more readily enables the real to be distinguished from the counterfeit.

Mrs. Walton had of late imagined that their obsequious attentions were paid, not out of love, but from a covetous desire to become the inheritors of her fortune, and she had determined to defeat that object.

A few weeks before the attack of paralysis, to which we have referred, she had drawn up her will, and had bequeathed the whole of her property, real and personal, to her sister's son, Frank Atherton, with the exception of a small annuity, which she desired should be paid to her servant. The will was witnessed by two friends in London, whom Mrs. Walton visited for the purpose, without their being aware of the contents, and was afterwards placed beneath the cover of an old Bible in the secret recess of an antique chest of drawers, which stood in her private apartment.

For months Mrs. Walton continued to linger, sometimes rallying for a short time, and then relapsing into her former condition.

And Christmas was for the third time approaching

since her attack, and with its approach a strange foreboding that this would be her last on earth, found a
place in her heart.

This feeling she made known to Frank, who had
called upon her, and had, out of genuine affection and
compassion, endeavoured in many ways to lighten her
suffering.

She had become quite resigned to her fate, and the
only regret which escaped her was that she was to be
separated from the nephew, who in a thousand ways had
become endeared to her. "Frank," she whispered one
morning, "you appear to have some burden upon your
mind. I have remarked this during your last few visits,
and I would fain comfort my motherless boy, and help
him out of his difficulty whatever it may be. Will you
not take me into your confidence, and by so doing
furnish me with one more opportunity of at least soothing
your care with my sympathy, if I may not have the
power to remove it entirely from your shoulders?"

"Dear aunt, you do not, I hope, for a moment doubt
that I would gladly confide in you—you who have ever
treated me with all the gentleness of a mother, and have
guided me by your counsel and tender chiding. No!
no! I will tell you all that disturbs my heart at
the present moment. The foreboding which you have

mentioned to me has not, you may readily imagine, tended to make me joyful, and this, taken with the fact that I have become enamoured with a lady whose affections, after what has transpired, I can scarcely hope to gain, will be sufficient to explain my dejection."

"Her name, Frank?"

"May Jeffries," replied Frank, in a voice trembling with the emotion which the mention of that dear name excited.

"Ah! the daughter of that good man, Squire Jeffries. I have seen her—a slender, gentle girl of about eighteen summers. If her disposition is as sweet as her face, then indeed she will be a prize worth the winning."

"Frank, my boy, you have forgotten the old saying, 'faint heart never yet won fair lady.' If I remember rightly, you mentioned, when you entered the room, that you had some business to transact with Squire Jeffries; that being so, I would advise you to go at once to him. The day is not yet far advanced, and if you succeed in pleasing him, he will, I feel certain, from what I have heard of his character, invite you to spend the evening with him. You know the rest. I think nothing of the affair to which you have alluded, and if Miss Jeffries be the lady I judge her to be, she will treat it as lightly as I do. Go, Frank, and may success attend you. If it does not to-night, you may rest assured that I will leave no stone unturned to bring about what you desire. Ah, Frank, you do not know what a determined woman is capable of. Your cause will be safe with me, though I may appear by my present condition to be placed *hors de jeu.*"

Frank, after wishing Mrs. Walton good day, and promising to inform her at the earliest possible moment of the result of his visit to Squire Jeffries, quitted the house, and made his way towards the home of the genial Squire and his winsome daughter. On his way thither he was accosted by Mr. Dove and Charles, who were about to pay a visit to Mrs. Walton. These gentlemen, who had always treated Frank with the greatest coolness, appeared to be on this occasion quite affable. They seemed to have discovered some hidden virtues in him which led them to covet his acquaintance, and to be quite anxious that he should think well of them. Would he not come and spend the Christmas with them. They had determined to have good company and to spend the festive season in the most congenial manner. Would he not make one of the party; they would indeed be happy if they could induce him to do so. It had many times occurred to them to ask him, but owing to business matters, and one thing and another, they had unfortunately omitted to do so. He must pardon their seeming want of courtesy, and allow them the opportunity of atoning for the past.

Frank felt quite staggered at this unexpected outburst of friendly feeling, for he saw not the serpent which lay concealed beneath the flowers of their rhetoric, and would, perhaps, have acceded to their solicitations, had it not been somewhat uncertain whether, in the event of his accepting, he would be able to fulfil his promise. He thanked them much for the polite invitation with which they had honoured him, but, as he could not at the moment give a definite answer, he would write to them on his return to Liverpool.

Frank then passed onwards, and in a short time found himself at Squire Jeffries, with what result we have already learned.

Had he seen the malicious look which was cast after him by the men who had but that day been plotting how to remove him from their path, and who now professed the greatest friendship for him, he would not have walked in so sprightly a way, and with such an air of contentment, and joyful expectancy. 'Tis a wise and merciful Providence which hides from men the events of the future which are to disturb and darken their individual life, and there is in truth a "blissful

c

ignorance," which tends much to secure the enjoyments of the present.

"Charles," said Mr. Dove, clapping him on the back a few moments after parting from Frank, "we have done an excellent stroke of business; we have disarmed the foe, and in doing so, have removed the only weight which oppressed my mind, and tended to lower the scale of circumstances on the side of misfortune. If young Atherton should by any possible means escape from the clutches of Jerry Mills, he will not now for a moment suspect that we are implicated in the matter. Not that I think there is any fear of his doing so, because I see that Jerry is a man who is well versed in the business he has undertaken, and one from whom it would be next to an impossibility to escape. Whilst, however, there is the slightest chance of a contingency arising, it is well to secure ourselves, and having now done so, I feel fifty per cent. the better. Just to cap the day, I think we will call upon Mrs. Walton, and see what we can do to ease her sufferings." As he said this, an unmistakable look passed between him and Charles, a look which had in it a strange commingling of hate and joy.

And the twilight rolled onwards, with shadows ever increasing in their density, and the air seemed filled with the stillness which breathes upon the soul "the calm of evening, sublimely tender, solemnly serene."

There was peace on all around—and yet, no; there were human beings in the midst of all this harmony of Nature whose hearts were rocking to and fro on the turbulent waves of sin. Would those waves sweep into destruction the frail, covetous barques which laboured over them, or would they carry them into the haven of rest and gladness?

CHAPTER IV.

WE must now return to Frank, whom it will be remembered we left *en route* to Bidston Hill. On reaching the Landing Stage he crossed the river by the Woodside boat, and then directed his steps towards the East Float, at one corner of which he hoped to be able to hire a small rowing boat. The evening promising to be a fine one, he anticipated a pleasant row as far as Poulton Bridge, from which place he would walk briskly, for the air was keen and frosty, to the summit of the hill, and then wander at random amongst the fine gorse and heather which clothe its sides, and give to it that peculiar charm and attraction which, with the fine and extensive view obtainable there on clear days, render it so favoured a resort.

Boats there were plenty, and soon Frank was gliding up the Float, with merry heart and with eyes sparkling

with the fire which was generated by the healthy exercise,
and the joyful thoughts which May's letter had awakened.
He did not dream of the danger which hovered near him;
his thoughts were of her he loved so intensely, and who
had now—could it be really so, or was it but a dream
which his fevered imagination had produced, and which
his longing spirit would fain model into a reality—by
her manner and encouraging note shown him that his
feelings were warmly reciprocated?

Meanwhile, Jerry Mills and his comrades had not
been idle, and had noted, with much satisfaction, the
course Frank had taken. They had followed closely,
taking care not to attract the attention of Frank; and
on reaching the Float they proceeded to the south-west
corner, where a small fleet of coal flats lay moored, like
sombre spectres on the dark, dusty water. The master
of one of these—a friend of Jerry's—would, no doubt,
lend them his punt, and by this means they would be
able to follow without exciting the least suspicion in the
mind of Frank.

They were clever villains! Jerry had, as he observed
the tactics of their intended prey, whispered in hoarse
tones, which told but too plainly that his bad nature
was now thoroughly aroused, words to the effect that if
they engaged an ordinary pleasure boat, such as that

which Frank had taken, their appearance would be
incongruous, and might easily betray them; but that if
they could obtain a large punt it would seem as if they
were pursuing their ordinary avocation.

Opportunely it occurred to Jerry that his friend, the
master of the "William and Mary," was in the locality,
and would doubtless oblige him with a punt.   In this
he was not mistaken; and giving as his reason for
requiring the boat, that he and his friends were going
"to do a pleasant little bit o' bisness at the top o' the
Float, and to have p'raps a bit o' a spree at the Pool
Inn," he jumped in, followed by his men, pushed off
from the wharf, and sculled after Frank, whose boat,
yielding to his powerful strokes, was rapidly drawing
near to its destination.

At first they could not quite agree as to how they
should proceed.   One of the ruffians, Bill Bouncer,
thought that as the day was rapidly waning, they might
venture to intercept Frank's boat.   "Run into it, acci-
dental like," said he, leering, "and when the cove's in
the water hit him on the nut with this y'ere boat-hook.
This y'ere punt 'll be none the worse fur the scrimmage,
and then the bisness will be done;" and, he added,
in mock theatrical tones, "If 'twere done, when 'tis
done, then 't were well it were done quickly."   "Yer

edication's improving," said Jerry, laughing at the sally
made by Bouncer, "but there's too much risk o' dis
kivery about the thing. My motter is 'slow but sure;
if yer feels inclined to go in fur them high-fangled
noshuns. No, no; we'll wait a bit. Jerry hasn't no
hankering fur to burn his fingers. Yer see, Bill, if we
tried your plan, the body would be rekivered. Yes, to
be sure it would. And then, yer knows, what might
foller. Jerry wasn't born yesterday, or the day afore
neither, nor no how, and, if he could prufecy, he'd say
as how that young cove was going on the hill, and as
how he were just going to walk into our arms as a lamb
might do into the fold." "Bravo, Jerry," said Tom
Bully, the third ruffian, "yer right, and Bill's wrong—
there's my fist on it."

But Jerry's "lamb-like" prophecies were to be dispelled
like snow before a breeze from the sunny south, and in
his person he was to carry a perpetual reminder that
appearances are sometimes deceptive. They calculated
upon gaining their end without difficulty, and without a
struggle, but they were to be grievously disappointed.
Frank, strong and courageous, would not fall into their
hands so easily as they expected; and even if they were
to be successful in their attempt upon his life, it would
not be without the exercise of all their crafty ingenuity
and brutal force.

As Frank's boat grated against the wall adjoining Poulton Bridge, the twilight merged into the deeper shades of evening, and the moon, robed in her resplendent beauty, came forth once more to spread abroad her tender, refining influence.

The moon, with her translucent light, has ever been associated with tales of love, and, indeed, her fair unwrinkled face seems always to look with complacency and approval upon the pranks of that arch urchin, Cupid. Longfellow speaks of her as "the symbol of love in heaven;" and Frank, as he gazed upon her, and experienced again that strange, sweet whispering in his heart, "Peace, all will be well, May shall be yours, and your future shall be all that you anticipate and desire," could have expatiated with poetic ardour upon her queenly splendour, and told how her silvery beams waked to ecstacy the music of his heart.

After securing the boat, Frank made for Bray Head Cottage, which stands near the crest of the hill, passing on his way the spot where once stood the summer-house in which Monmouth met his brother conspirators prior to the rebellion. As he was much in advance of the trio, there was no possibility of their intercepting him before he reached the cottage mentioned. Here he would partake of some refreshment; and, being somewhat of an antiquarian, would endeavour to elicit from the proprietor of the cottage, an intellectual man, Urmson by name, whose ancestors had lived on the hill for ages past, some of the folk-lore of the neighbourhood. Arriving, he sat down before the cheerful fire in the kitchen to an ample repast, and old Urmson, being in a chatty humour, remained with him; and, in answer to Frank's enquiries, went on to say, in his quaint style :—"Aye, aye, there be not many tales connected with the hill. When a boy, I did hear that it and the surrounding district was invaded by hobgoblins."

"What are those?" asked Frank.

"In form," continued Urmson, "they be something like horses, I am told, but I never have seen any. They used to be all over the place, sometimes near the windmill, and at night they would leave their haunts and commit some depredation, happen kill a bullock, or at other times, I have heard say, they've ploughed fields, much to the astonishment and good fortune of the farmer, who on waking some morning found that his work was already done for him. Then there be an old story about Bidston Hall. Have you no heard it?"

Frank confessed his ignorance. adding that he should very much like to hear the details.

"Aye, aye," continued Urmson, "it's many years ago, but I hear say that even at the present day can be seen in Bidston Hall the marks left on the hall flags by the ghost."

"Ghost!" said Frank, involuntarily drawing his chair nearer to the fire, not that he had any belief in, or dread of, those creations of ignorance and childish fancy, but from the mysterious feelings which the mention of the name ghost seems ever to excite.

"Aye, aye, ghost. The inmates of the Hall be aforetimes often terrified at the strange, peculiar noises which be heard during night time, and even the villagers shuddered and increased their speed if occasion required them to pass in the vicinity after nightfall. Aye! aye! but we have no heard lately about the ghost." "Ah!" said Frank, "perhaps it is only biding its time until some imaginative novelist rouses the echoes and slumbering spirits with a thrilling tale, entitled the 'Ghost of Bidston Hall;' and then again there will be mysterious rustlings and sighings, a smell of brimstone, and a gathering round the ancient fire-place in the half-light to watch the blue flames flicker in and about the chimney, and to whisper old, old stories of long ago."

At this moment Frank happening to turn his head

from the fire into which he had been gazing, thought he
noticed a dark, savage-looking face peering in through the
window, but, as on taking a nearer view he could not
see anybody, he thought it must have been some fancy
arising out of the subject of the conversation.

"Has there ever been a murder committed on the
Hill?" asked Frank. The question, doubtless, being suggested by the face he had pictured looking in upon
him.

"Murder!" repeated Urmson, in a thoughtful tone.
"No, I never heard tell of one, and more, it is prophecied that there never shall be one in this vicinity."

"Prophecied by whom?" asked Frank.

"By Nixon," responded Urmson. In a small book
published by him, he calls Bidson 'God's Croft,' and if
it be so, how could there possibly be so foul a crime
perpetrated here?"

"But many beautiful spots of God's earth have been
desecrated by sins as foul as that of murder," soliloquized
Frank, as he reached his hat, and made preparations for
his departure. "Good night, Mr. Urmson, and thank
you for the interesting particulars you have given to me.
I hope soon to be able to pay you another visit, when
we will resume the topic upon which we have been
talking this evening. I see you have some very old

books in manuscript upon your shelves bearing upon the neighbourhood, which, doubtless, will afford me some pleasure to peruse." "Aye, aye; those old books were kept by my forefathers. Good night."

"Good night," reiterated Frank, and hurried forth.

Wandering hither and thither, pondering over the one subject which now engrossed his thoughts, he came to the wicket-gate, which stands at the entrance to the pathway leading to the village, and here he loitered awhile to enjoy the splendid view of the old Church of St. Oswald and the homesteads nestling in the valley, which, in the clear moonlight, presented indeed a scene of rustic beauty. So wrapt in thought was he, that he heard not the stealthy footsteps of the three dark figures creeping towards him 'neath the shadow of the wall, and wandering on, he came to Summerhouse Hill, and to that dark avenue which leads to Bidston Road. Turning, he was about to proceed down the avenue in question, when he was startled by a strange noise behind him, and looking round, found himself confronted by three ruffians in menacing attitude.

Frank being unarmed, and so completely surprised, knew scarcely what action to take. As it would have been madness to think of opposing such odds, Frank's first idea was naturally flight, and the prevailing darkness

seemed to favour such a project; but a moment's reflection shewed him how futile such an attempt would be.
" Down with him, lads," cried Jerry, advancing, and
levelling a tremendous stroke at Frank. Stepping hastily
aside to avoid Jerry's murderous cudgel, and now divining
clearly the intention of his assailants, Frank, without a
moment's further hesitation, dealt Jerry a frightful blow
on his enormous nose, breaking that florid organ of re-
spiration, and felling its owner like an ox. The attack
on his part was so sudden as to completely confuse
Jerry's associates, and before they were able to recover
themselves, Frank had dashed his fist into the face of
each with terrible force and result. Then veering round,
he essayed to make good his escape, but the ruffians
pounced upon him before he could do so. Fighting
with the desperation of a man who feels that his life
is at stake, and with the double strength which that
desperation supplies, Frank, though half stunned and
bleeding from a wound he had received in the head,
appeared for some moments to be gaining an advantage.
By this time, however, Jerry had gathered himself
together, and, seeing the state of affairs, he rushed at
Frank, clasped him round the legs and threw him
violently to the ground, whilst, with oaths and curses,
the others closed upon him.

Frank, in falling, clung to Jerry, and, fighting like madmen, they rolled over and over one another, Jerry savagely snarling and muttering dreadful imprecations, until a blow on the head from a large stone left Frank, bleeding and senseless, quite at the mercy of his merciless antagonists.

And all was still and dark. Save the occasional crackling of a twig, the sighing of the night wind, and the rustling feathers of some bird aroused from its slumber by the recent struggle, not a sound was heard. The moon, fearful of being the witness of a crime so foul, had disappeared from view behind a heavy cloud, which, propelled by the northern breeze, was rapidly spreading itself over the horizon, and which, in its density, seemed to scowl down upon the reckless trio, and to threaten them with the terrible vengeance of heaven.

The ruffians, after dealing what they thought was a fatal blow, had pushed Frank's body to the darkest side of the avenue, where they themselves retired to listen if the sounds of the recent struggle had been heard by any wanderer on the hill, and whether anyone was hastening to the place from whence the sounds proceeded.

Having satisfied themselves that this was not so, they

bound up their wounds; and then, raising Frank from the ground and carrying him between them, they made their way back to the Float, taking care to avoid the public highway, lest they should be discovered and brought to justice.

Once, when necessity compelled them to cross the road, they were startled by the approach of two men. Hastily placing Frank in an upright position, and supporting him thus, they grouped themselves and made it appear that they were engaged in earnest conversation.

The strangers drew nearer and nearer, until they were within a few yards of where Jerry and his companions stood, when they paused, without apparent cause for so doing, and much to the consternation of Jerry, who, with his guilty conscience, imagined that the men had got some inkling of the crime he and his associates had been committing. Grasping his cudgel, and whispering a hasty word of caution to his friends, he placed himself before Frank to cover him from observation, and then awaited the result.

But the men passed on with a polite "Good evening," and were soon lost to sight in the surrounding gloom.

Breathing freely again, Jerry gave the word "forrard," and getting into motion, they succeeded in reaching their boat without further cause for apprehension.

Laying Frank at the bottom of the boat, they pushed off quietly, Jerry remarking, "Take yer time now, Bill; it wants three hours to high water, and the gates will no be opened yet fur a hour. We must run through into the river at all risks."

Silently and slowly the boat moved onwards in its course, its occupants speaking but little, and that little but in low hoarse whispers. As for Frank, he had remained so quiet and motionless that the men imagined he would never recover consciousness. And what benefit would it be to him to recover his senses, seeing that he was entirely in the power of three men who were determined, at all hazards, to deprive him of his life; would it not rather be better that he should die in this unconscious, painless condition, than that he should suffer the terrors of drowning to arrive at the same end? But Frank's time to "depart" had not yet arrived; a wise and kind Providence was watching over him; the arm that moves the world was moved with compassion and tender protecting love in his behalf, and these wild, lawless men might do their utmost to kill him, might hope, and strive, and plot, but all in vain. Man cannot defeat the purposes of God. There is an old adage that "a friend in need is a friend indeed;" and truly, if like Frank we make friends with God, then we may confidently rely upon having a friend near to us in all life's trials and necessities, and one who is not only near, but also able, willing, and ready to aid and protect us.

Awaiting their opportunity, and covered by the darkness, Jerry and his company succeeded in passing through the dock gates into the river, without exciting any attention, and then turning the boat's head to the tide, they essayed to make their way to Jerry's smack, which lay moored off New Brighton. As the tide was swift, and the wind kept increasing in force every minute, this was a task which required a strenuous effort, and which would take some considerable time. "It'll be blowin' great guns shortly," said Jerry, "and we mustn't lose no time, or there's danger ahead—pull away, Bill!"

And the spray kept splashing over the side of the boat, and the waves kept increasing in height and volume each instant. Not a moment was to be lost if they were to reach their destination in safety. Their frail punt, heavily weighted as it was, could not live long in such a sea.

Jerry, who sat in the stern, kept her head well on to the waves, and, although he spoke words of encouragement to his comrades, his heart quailed when he gazed at the lowering heavens and the heavy sea.

The cool air, and the spray which dashed over

Frank, had a beneficial effect upon him, and tended to bring him back to consciousness.

Gradually, very gradually, he recovered. At first he could not understand his position, but, as his brain became less influenced by the stupor into which it had been so suddenly thrown, the events of the recent struggle crowded in upon him, and as he listened to the voices of those who were near him, the fact that he was now in the power of his assailants dawned upon him.

"What could have been the motive of their attack?" he reasoned with himself. It certainly could not be theft, for they had not deprived him of his watch, and they would not in that case have gone to the trouble of removing him from the hill.

They must be going to drown him, and yet he did not remember that he had done anything to create an enemy who would not be satisfied with less than his life. Oh, how his head seemed to ache and swim, and his body to be racked with pain.

"Steady, steady," cried Jerry, in anxious tones, "or her'll be capsized; pull fur yer life, the tide is now with us; and in half-an-hour we'll be alongside o' the 'Saucy Poll.'"

"Steady, steady there," repeated Jerry, as a huge wave dashed over the side of the boat, half filling it.

"Bail away there, Tom, or we shall ——." The remainder of Jerry's speech was lost, as at that moment another wave, more terrible than the last, struck against the side of the boat, capsizing it, and leaving its occupants struggling in the water.

"Help! Help! Oh God, help!

But God's ear was closed to the voices of the villains battling amidst the mighty waves. The time for compassion and mercy was past, and now they must be abandoned to cruel, relentless fate. Down into the trough of the sea they went, fighting and struggling for dear life. Jerry being a splendid swimmer, had succeeded in getting astride of the upturned boat, but the others were not so fortunate. Twice his companions had essayed to follow his example, but each time they stretched out to grasp the punt it was washed away from them by the receding wave.

At last, half filled with water, and completely exhausted; they threw up their hands in wild despair, and crying piteously for help, sank beneath the waves, reappeared again, and once again, and then finally passed from time into eternity, an eternity which, for them, had nothing in it bright and promising, but was all dark and ill-foreboding.

Frank was not drowned, but how he and Jerry escaped that fate we must leave for another chapter to recount.

CHAPTER V.

I T was Christmas Eve, and Seaton Villa, the residence of Squire Jeffries, seemed to be smiling
out a welcome through its high bow windows to the
festive, joyous season. The old, old fashioned Christmas
appeared once again to be decking himself in his robe
of spotless white, and to be awaiting his opportunity to
bestow upon the expectant world a wealth of hearty
good cheer and comfort. His kind, genial smile robbed
the cold, icy cold air and snow of their keenness, and
found a reflection in almost every human heart. The
snow, at least, touched into rapture by a passing moon-
beam, shot out from its numerous crystals a sparkling
welcome, and seemed to be whispering softly :

    " Sing heigh ho ! the holly, the holly,
    " This life is most jolly, most jolly ;
    " This life is most jolly ! "

whilst the old villa, as it shed forth from its

windows a bright crimson light over the soft feathery snow, appeared to be echoing the sweet refrain. The inside of the villa had been transformed by May's fairy wand into a veritable enchanted castle, than which Oberon could boast no fairer. Evergreens and flowers, artistically arranged, had indeed worked wonders in the internal appearance of May's home, whilst she, with her lady friends, in gay attire, moving about, hither and thither, completed the interesting picture, and evoked many expressions of admiration from a group of the sterner sex, who, with the old Squire, were deciding as to a few charades for the evening. The Squire, particularly, was in good spirits, and had determined to make his friends spend the time right merrily.

"Nothing lovelier than woman!" he would exclaim, half apologetically, as he managed to secure some lady who, incautiously, ventured beneath the mistletoe, and imprinted upon her blushing cheek what the more youthful of the male sex present termed a "spanking" kiss. If, as was the case once or twice, the lady, divining his intentions, succeeded in getting from under the bough before the Squire could prevent her, he would still persist in having the kiss; and if, subsequently, the lady or any of his friends remarked that "it was not fair," he would laugh heartily, rub his hands together, as though on excellent terms with himself, and exclaim, "Old man's privilege! Old man's privilege!!"

Full of fun, which could not be contained, the old man exerted so happy an influence over his friends, that soon the whole of them were in excellent spirits, each doing his or her best to add to the general enjoyment.

As the evening advanced, however, it might be noticed that May at times looked somewhat anxious, and that she often approached the window which opened upon the avenue leading to the Hall, and peered out into the clear night as though watching for some one, who, unfortunately for her feelings, seemed bent upon disappointing her. "Why does he not come?" she murmured to herself, as she quitted her post at the window. "He said he would be delighted to spend the Christmas with us. Surely something must have happened to prevent him from coming—but then he ought to have written—he might have imagined that I would be anxious. There could have been no mistake in the invitation, because all the guests but he have arrived. Perhaps he will come early in the morning; and, now that I think of it, I believe I did not specifically mention that we should expect him on Christmas Eve. But I do wish he would come!"

At this moment the old Squire came up, and, caressing her, he said, "Come, come my little daughter, you appear somewhat out of spirits. You know you are the hostess to-night, and must be the life of the party as usual. Have all the guests arrived, May?" ."All but Mr. Atherton, father!" "And does that account for your despondency," he said, looking at her rather sharply. "Come, come—if he respects me at all, he will be here by to-morrow morning at the latest; and if he does not arrive, and sends no apology, then he is not the gentleman I take him to be, and is not worthy of further thought."

"But I cannot rid myself of the feeling that something serious may have happened to him," said May. "Last night I dreamt that I was sailing on a wide river, and that all was dark and terrible. Glancing over the side of the vessel, as we were hurried on by the storm, I imagined that I heard a voice faintly calling for help, and as I gazed, the moon, freed for an instant from the surrounding clouds, sent out a gleam of light over the dark waves, and there, drowning, I saw——I saw——."

"Surely not Mr. Atherton," said the Squire.

Yes, it was he," continued May, "and, what frightened me more, I fancied he was calling me by my name—

and then I awoke, feeling cold and half dead with fright."

"Tut, tut," said the Squire, "I shall imagine that you have fallen in love with Mr. Atherton soon. I have long since formed the opinion that people dream most of those subjects which are uppermost in their thoughts, and I must, therefore, conclude that my little daughter has been thinking more of Mr. Atherton than was good for her. I do not say anything in disparagement of the young man—indeed I rather like him, though," he added, teasingly, "I have not brought myself to think of him as a son-in-law,—but I do not place any reliance upon dreams."

"But still you must admit, father," said May, "that dreams often come true."

"I won't admit anything but that you are a silly little goose to think of such things," said the Squire. "Now go and join the company before your absence is commented upon." And, kissing her fondly, he trotted off to the library, where he and a few of the elderly guests had retired to discuss politics, and that great question of interest to all Manchester men, the proposed Ship Canal; also, for the purpose of giving more room to the young people, who were playing a few old-fashioned games in the drawing-room.

May rejoined her young friends, and soon the sad impressions which her dream and Frank's subsequent non-appearance had produced, had given way to the glad feelings which seemed to pervade the very atmosphere of the villa, and to sparkle out of the eyes of the merry group gathered beneath its hospitable roof.

May was yet, however, to feel the bitter pang of a dread uncertainty still more keenly. The morrow came, as fair a Christmas morn as any which e'er dawned upon mankind, but with it came no news of Frank— no news of the one who now seemed inexpressibly dear to her. She learned that she loved him, but with that knowledge, alas, there came the terrible thought that he had met with some fearful accident, which would for ever remove him from her presence.

Again the merry laugh resounded, and the Squire's mahogany creaked and groaned beneath the pile of good things which a kindly heart had provided, and of which an appreciative company partook.

The evening approached, and the guests were gathered round the huge fire in the drawing-room, inventing "patchwork" stories, and amusing themselves in various other ways, when suddenly there came a loud knocking at the hall door. May started involuntarily, and her breath came and went in rapid succession. A voice was then heard asking for Mr. Atherton, and, as the Squire caught the name, he started forward and requested the enquirer to enter. By the light of the hall lamp, May recognised Betsy, the faithful old servant of Mrs. Walton, who, in answer to the Squire's questions, informed him and May, who had also drawn near, that . Mrs. Walton, Mr. Atherton's aunt, had become very much worse in health, indeed so unwell that the doctor had opined that she might die at any moment. This being so, and knowing from a letter she had received a few days ago from her nephew, that he had accepted the invitation of Squire Jeffries to spend the Christmas with him, she had sent for him in order that, in her few remaining hours on earth, she might be comforted by his presence.

"You have surely not left Mrs. Walton alone!" said the squire.

"Oh, no! Of course the doctor is with her—then there are her relations, the Doves, and old Mrs. Simkins, the nurse," replied Betsy.

"But Mr. Atherton, although he accepted our invitation, has neither put in an appearance nor sent word to explain the cause of his absence. I hope nothing has happened to him. If there had, I should have thought that his father would have at once informed

Mrs. Walton. We are, I must confess, rather concerned about him, and more so now that he might have been a source of solace to your mistress. Kindly say how exceedingly sorry my daughter and I are to hear of her deplorable condition. Can we do anything to ease her sufferings, do you think? Should my daughter return with you to see if she can render any assistance?" asked the Squire.

"Thank you; I think not," replied Betsy, "but I will convey your message to my mistress."

Betsy then retired, and in a short time arrived at her mistress's dwelling. She was met in the drawing-room by Mr. Dove, who informed her that Mrs. Walton had become much worse, and that the doctor desired that no one but the nurse should remain with him in the room. He would convey her message to the doctor, who would in turn inform Mrs. Walton, if she were indeed in a condition to receive any message.

It is necessary here to explain that Frank's father, on finding that his son did not return to his home on the evening he set out for Bidston, had become exceedingly anxious about him, and as day after day passed without tidings of the missing one, he had been prostrated by the fear which racked his brain and heart. He had set the police to work, and had telegraphed to all the friends and places he knew Frank visited.

A telegram had, therefore, in due course been sent
to Mrs. Walton, but this had been cunningly intercepted
by Mr. Dove. Expecting something would speedily result from the interview he had had with Jerry Mills, he
had closely watched for communications addressed to
Mrs. Walton, from Liverpool, and how far he succeeded
in his object we already know. In replying to the telegram, as from Mrs. Walton, he said: "Frank has not
been to see me within the last seven or eight days. I
am very anxious about him, but trust that no misfortune has happened. Pray write to me as soon as you
glean any information respecting his whereabouts."

Neither telegram nor reply was, however, shewn to Mrs.
Walton, for reasons which were best known to Mr. Dove,
and now he dismissed Betsy, in order that he might the
more readily vary the answer she had received, so as to
create no suspicion in the mind of his dying relative.

Mr. Dove had some slight idea that Mrs. Walton
knew of the covetous regard he had for her possessions,
and this, coupled with the fear that she might connect
him and Charles in some way with the mysterious
disappearance of her favourite nephew, doubtless made
him most anxious to conceal the fact.

He, therefore, approached the bed upon which Mrs.
Walton lay, and whispered to her:—"Frank has not yet

arrived at Squire Jeffries', but as soon as he puts in an appearance he will be informed of your wish."

Mrs. Walton turned upon him a searching look, as though she would read what was passing in his very soul, and then sighed and said in broken accents:— "Frank—Frank—I—wish—you—would—come—Oh !— I—cannot—breathe—open—the—window—give—me—air air—air—O—this—weight—tell—Frank—I—leave—him— all—my—Will—all—" and here the voice ceased, and Mrs. Walton's lifeless body fell back upon the bed. A bright, heavenly smile, reflective of the pure light which clothed her soul, settled upon her countenance, and fixed itself there as though to tell the world of the welcome she had given to, and received from, the angelic messengers who had come to convey her spirit home. A well spent life and a saving faith had secured for her a future that, in prospective, was radient with promise, and, in possession, was full to overflowing with joy unutterable and full of glory. No wonder then that, brightened with heavenly grace, she could repeat, a few days prior to her decease:—

> " O Death, no more, no more delay,
> " My spirit longs to flee away,
>   " And be at rest;
> " The will of Heaven my will shall be,—
> " I bow to the divine decree,
>   " To God's behest."

Her end was peace, sweet, sublime peace, and the simple and touching story of her life was recorded in letters of gold by the angels in God's book of remembrance.

Her last words had reached but the ear of Mr. Dove, the nurse and doctor having for the moment retired to an ante-room to prepare a stimulant for the dying woman, and he knew but too well how to conceal them.

Mr. Dove now assumed the entire management of all Mrs. Walton's affairs, and took up his residence at the villa, in order that he might, as he affirmed, the more readily attend to the necessary arrangements in connection with the funeral.

When all was quiet, and the night somewhat advanced, Mr. Dove rose from his couch, and lighting a candle, he entered Mrs. Walton's private apartment, and proceeded to ransack the whole of the drawers with the object of finding the Will to which that lady referred in her last moments. His search, however, proving fruitless, he came to the conclusion that no Will had been prepared; and this idea was strengthened when he thought again of the words used by Mrs. Walton—"I leave all to Frank—my will." "Yes; yes! I see it all now clearly," he muttered. "She has made none, or she would not have troubled to tell me that she left the whole of her fortune to Frank—curse him—but no—there is no necessity to do that now. Jerry has effectually settled him, that's certain, from what he told Charles—and now all, all will be mine."

"I will send for my lawyer to-morrow and get the matter arranged as speedily as possible. When I obtain the money I will sell up quietly through my friend in London, and leave the country and my creditors to shift for themselves."

And his face glowed with the fiendish delight his seeming success had aroused; and, chuckling, he extinguished the light, and gave himself up—not to sleep—but to meditation—a meditation the fair prospects of which were, however, marred and distorted by the occasional awakening of his slumbering conscience.

A week passed, and all that remained of Mrs. Walton had been committed to mother earth.

Betsy had been summarily disposed of; that is to say, cast upon the world with but one month's wages, and with her advanced age as an almost insurmountable object in the way of her procuring such employment as would secure to her the means of sustenance; and the villa had been deprived of its furniture and interior

The various articles which had tended so much to
beautify Mrs. Walton's residence were removed to Mr.
Dove's mansion, there to remain until the date of the
contemplated sale.

Meanwhile, Mr. Dove's lawyer had been busy, and
to some purpose. In the course of a few months the
whole of Mrs. Walton's estate, including the amount
realized by the sale of the villa, had been secured to
Mr. Dove, and as Charles had assisted him in procuring
it, he divided it equally with him. A slightly favourable
turn in his business had for a time averted the
impending catastrophe, and thus tended the more to
secure the object he had in view.

Squire Jeffries and May learned with deep regret
of the decease of Frank's aunt; and as they had heard
nothing as to the whereabouts of Frank personally, the
Squire determined to take May to Liverpool, in the
hope of dispelling the despondency which had taken
possession of her. The Squire had learned her secret,
and with tender solicitation he endeavoured to comfort
her and to bring again the cheerful smile and the
warm glowing colour to her pale, anxious face.

They arrived in Liverpool at the commencement of
the New Year, and after engaging apartments in the
Adelphi Hotel, they had proceeded to Mr. Atherton's

place of business. Here they learned from the manager the story of Frank's disappearance, and coupled with it the sad fact that the uncertainty of his fate had preyed so much on the mind of his father as to completely deprive him of his reason.

The good old Squire was, as may be imagined, very much concerned at the sad turn events had taken; and in order to assist in the recovery of Mr. Atherton, he had succeeded in persuading that gentleman's friends to allow him to be conveyed to Crompton. Here he would have the benefit of the fine country air, and would be tended by May; in short, would receive every attention that it was possible to bestow and that was necessary to ensure his restoration.

When, therefore, the Squire and May, both very much dispirited, returned to their home, it was in company with Mr. Atherton, the strong man now reduced by the loss of mind to the harmless and helpless condition of an infant.

But what had become of Frank? What dangers had he passed through, and what hardships had he endured? What had happened to Jerry Mills, and how were his schemes and plots against the Doves progressing?

These are questions which require to be speedily solved.

CHAPTER VI.

FRANK, fully aroused by his sudden transition from the boat into the cold waves of the Mersey, and by the sense of the danger he was in, made every possible effort to keep himself afloat. Being a swimmer, he succeeded in doing so for some time, but the battle, it was evident, would not be a prolonged one. The swimmer's diminished strength, and the violence of the storm, if no succour was at hand, must soon determine the issue disastrously for our hero.

The experiences of his life were crowded into a moment's duration, and flashed like a meteor across his excited brain, a darkness seemed to be gathering in his eyes; his limbs, benumbed with cold, ceased to move, and, with a piteous cry for help, he surrendered himself to his fate.

But this time help was near.

Just when humanity, tossed and buffetted on the waves of adverse circumstances, is about to yield up the last supporting hope, coy Mercy, the fair Angel of Providence, comes upon the scene, and, with well-timed movement, snatches the despairing one back to life, to love, and hope.

The moon again shone out upon the dark waters, and providentially revealed the struggling form to the crew of a passing vessel. One of the sailors on board, a brave, dauntless fellow, quickly tied the end of a rope around his body, and giving the other end to those on board, he seized a life buoy, sprang on to the side of the vessel, and plunged into the turbulent waters which washed her sides.

Rising to the surface, and aided by the light of the moon, he swam towards Frank, seized him by the hair, just as he was sinking beneath the waves, passed the life buoy under his arms, and then, with a wild hurrah, the sailors heaved up the line.

As Frank and his rescuer rose to the level of the deck, many a kind and succouring hand was laid upon them, and, with almost less time than it takes to recount the incident, they were conveyed to the cabin, and restoratives were applied to Frank's inanimate form.

For some time the efforts of the friendly mariners

were apparently fruitless, but after almost exhausting the varied means at their disposal, they were rewarded by the signs of returning consciousness.

But Frank was yet to undergo the virulence of a fever, brought on by the terrible sufferings to which he had been subjected through the dastardly attempt upon his life. Long after the storm which so furiously lashed the ocean, and breathed out destruction in its wild, fitful gasps had subsided, the storm, which tossed upon its billows Frank's mental and physical faculties, continued to rage with unabated strength.

The vessel which had so opportunely for our hero passed whilst he was struggling in the sea, was the "Andromeda," a German barque, of 1,200 tons register, bound for Melbourne.

She seemed a fine, graceful boat, as she glided over the waves with a swan-like motion, and her captain, Johann Winkelstein, a tall, broad-shouldered man, with a pleasing and attractive countenance, looked well fitted to be her commander. Captain Winkelstein was a man of about forty summers, with a heart as kind and brave as any which e'er beat beneath a sailor's jacket. Whenever his duties allowed, he would be found sitting near Frank, anticipating his wants, and watching over him with all the tenderness of a father.

"Vat can er mean mit zee vort May!" he would remark in his broken English, as some unconnected words escaped from Frank's frenzied lips one afternoon when the captain was bending over him. "Alvays, alvays May; vell, vell, May is von splendide months. Ach! how stupide I vas be—er speaks of one Mädchen!! So! so! dat ist der mystery to zee whole clue—so—so mein Burschen!! Ach, dese girls are zee cause fon much trouble! Potztausend! It brings me back to zee time ven I, as zee song says, 'mit zee lovely Wilhelmina passed zee happy hours avay.' I vell remember how vee met at zee Schutzenfest in Rosenheim. Her lovely face was von bouquet of smiles, und mine heart vas leap mit joy ven it caught zee sweet reflection—und how vee flirted, und—ach, vy avaken memories vich are so much mingled mit regret. Potztausend! dat fellow Schwartz, mit his coaxing und veedling vays, vas too much mit mine sweet girl not to veedle me fon her affection. But zare is zee old, old failing, vy can I not her false image fon mine heart rub off"—and he drew his hand across his eyes, to wipe away a tear which had welled up from the fountain of feeling within. "It must be as zee Irish poet says, "Zee heart dat has truly loved, loves on to zee close."

At this moment Frank turned upon his couch, and in doing so, disturbed the Captain's reverie.

"Where am I?" asked Frank, staring wildly around, as he raised himself on one elbow and vainly endeavoured to get out of the bunk in which he had been placed. " On board zee 'Andromeda,' bound for Melbourne," replied the captain, in his deep voice. "But you must remain kvite still; you have been very unwell. Ach—so—dat is besser," he added, as he gently laid Frank down and covered him with a warm blanket.

A few uneventful weeks glided slowly by—weeks which, to one with an active temperament like Frank's, were prone to induce feelings of fretfulness and impatience, but weeks of enforced inactivity in which, thanks to the kind attentions bestowed upon him by Captain Winkelstein, was to be gathered the strength needful to enable our hero to endure the dangers yet to cross his path. It would seem as if Nature, debarred from its rest, the fallow season, had now determined to assert its laws and sway by depriving Frank of the means wherewith to resist its operations. There would yet be time for the exercise of that manly form and vigour; yet be opportunities for the display of those kindly emotions which warmed his breast; yet be occasions for the elucidating of those convictions respecting things spiritual and temporal which gave force and character to a nature deeply susceptible to the distinctions between right and wrong.

Let not the vigorous mind chafe when some un-
foreseen circumstance compels relaxation from mental
pursuits, but rather let it with thankfulness receive the
benefit of the rest which a wise and prescient Providence
has seen fit to ordain.

One day as Frank was slowly pacing the deck, thinking over the events which had of late disturbed the
"even tenor of his way," and had been followed by
this terrible separation from those he loved, his thoughts
again, as on many occasions during the past two or
three weeks, turned homewards. How did his father
reconcile his absence? What reason had Squire Jeffries
and May assigned for his non-appearance at their home
at Christmas—a Christmas which, alas, had been passed
by him in suffering and mental aberration! What
steps had been taken to ascertain his whereabouts?
What had become of the villains who had committed
the outrage upon him, and what could have been the
motive which prompted them to seek his destruction?

Frank could not tell. The more he considered the
points, the more confused he became. There seemed
to be no gleam of light struggling through the dense
darkness in which the events of the past two months
had been crowded. "Vell, vell, vat you was be tinking
of so seriously?" said the captain, patting him on the

shoulder, and looking at him with a pleasant smile. "Zee old ting, I suppose. Vell, vell, I have been tinking too, and I fancy I see through zee plot fon vich you are zee victim."

"Captain, you always bring with you the same glad, welcome influence which a bright sunbeam does upon a wintry day!" ejaculated Frank, as he caught and returned the reflection of the captain's smile. "Potztausend, vy not—a pleasant look costs me nothing und gains me much—vy ven I was be on zee shore I vill vet dat I makes ten people a day good humoured simply mit mine smiles,

> Und ven I vas be on zee sea,
> Vy all dem smiles comes back to me."

"You are quite a poet," said Frank, laughingly interrupting him, "and also, I fancy a little speculative, because you evidently expect your action to augment your own happiness."

"No speculation at all," rejoined the captain. "It is a bisniss vich from its constitution can but yield large profits, und vich I recommends everybody vishing for true pleasure to engage in."

"But what is it you think you have discovered respecting the attempt upon my life?" said Frank.

"Vell," continued the captain, thoughtfully, "I believe

dat some other fellow is in love mit zee sweet May, about voom you so often speak in your illness, und he vishes to get you out of zee vay."

"Ah, then I have been letting out my secrets in my illness," said Frank, "it is well, perhaps, that I had nothing on my conscience, the revelation of which would bring the blush of shame to my face. But you are wrong, captain,—there is but one person besides you and myself who is aware of my attachment to Squire Jeffries' daughter. Not even to the lady herself have I declared my affection."

"Und zee other person who knows is?" queried the captain.

"My aunt, Mrs. Walton, a kind, dear lady, who since the death of my mother, and her own isolation from those of her kin, has taken quite a motherly interest in me."

"Une vere does she live?" asked the captain.

"But a short distance from Squire Jeffries, at Crompton," rejoined Frank. "You would be charmed, captain," he continued, "if you saw the beautiful surroundings, her handsome châlet, the neatly arranged gardens; and still more so if you could but catch a glimpse of that beauty of mind which guides and influences her in her dealings with those around her. Unfortunately, however, she has been laid aside by a serious illness during the last two or three years."

"She must be rich, then," said the captain, speaking in a low tone to himself.

"Yes, doubly so," chimed in Frank, "rich in a monetary sense, and wealthy in that which is more precious than rubies. Captain, I have often thought when I have been filled with aspirations after opulence and earthly honours, how transient the joy is after. all which these things afford; and at such times the text as to laying up treasures in heaven would come upon me with a convincing force quite irresistible."

"No doubt—no doubt"—said the captain meditatively, "but I am tinking I now see"—

"A mystery to zee whole clue," suggested Frank, laughingly.

"Yes, yes—this lady you say is rich, und takes von interest in you, and is unvell, is dat not so?"

"Yes!"

"So! Vell, has she not some other relations who visit her?" continued the captain, looking rather curiously at Frank.

"Yes," replied Frank, "there is a Mr. Dove and his son who pay great attention to my aunt, but I rather imagine she does not appreciate their endeavours. But what has all this to do with my case? It cannot have the slightest bearing upon it!"

"But," proceeded Captain Winkelstein, not heeding Frank's last remark, "how vas you received mit dese men; are dey alvays kind mit you, or do zey seem to be fretful ven you vas be mit dem?"

"What are you aiming at?" said Frank.

"Joost answer zee question!"

"Well, if I must, I must. These Doves and myself have never been very friendly together; indeed, I have always had some indescribable feeling of reluctance to be in their company. The last time I met them, however, they were exceedingly condescending, invited me to spend Christmas with them, and seemed as if they could not do sufficient to assure me of their kindly interest in my welfare."

"Ach so!—so! Und you do not tink it vood be gut mit dese shentlemens ven you vas be out of zee way, und dis lady vas to die?" said the captain, giving Frank a look that somewhat startled him, and which, taken in conjunction with the captain's words, dispelled any doubt which could exist as to his meaning.

"You do not mean to insinuate that?"——and here Frank stopped short, looked at the captain, and then commenced to pace the deck to and fro, to and fro, with his eyes vacantly regarding the sea.

"I'll vet von trifle zat dose shentlemens knows more about zee cause fon your absence dan dey vood like to disclose, and ven you vonce get back to England you vill, ven you vas be vise, go very carefully to vork. You must not announce your arrival to anybody until you have discovered the doings und condition fon your aunt und dese men, und den vee vill see vat vee vill see." So spake the captain; and Frank, who had eagerly listened to all that he had said, began to be impressed with the idea that the captain's suspicions were directed to the right quarter.

Had not Mrs. Walton on one occasion told him that she intended to make him her heir, and if he were removed, it was but reasonable to suppose that she would leave her fortune to the Doves, who were the only other relatives who visited her.

Frank disclosed this fact to the captain, and the more they talked the matter over, the more confirmed they became in their convictions.

Whilst they were thus engaged in earnest conversation, they noticed not the change which had suddenly taken place in the aspect of the weather. The waves of the Atlantic, which had during the day been unusually peaceful, now began to roll onwards in huge dark masses. Thick clouds appeared on the horizon, and the wind commenced whistling through the shrouds of the "Andromeda" in a sad, mysterious manner.

The captain's attention was soon drawn to the threatening danger by the heavy labouring of the vessel and the gathering darkness, but too late to avert the catastrophe which loomed above them.

"Reef zee sails," he cried, but before the order could be carried out a tremendous gust of wind caught them, rent them in shreds, and carried away a couple of the masts.

The vessel was thown upon her side, but she quickly righted again.

Then ensued a scene of confusion. Some of the men had been thrown into the sea by the accident, but fortunately they were soon rescued from their perilous position by those on board. Frank and the captain had saved themselves by clinging to the vessel's rail.

Hastily the debris was cleared from the deck, and preparations made for the erection of a jury-mast, but, owing to the violence of the storm, it was thought unadvisable to do anything further in that direction.

It is often remarked that troubles do not come singly, and certainly it seemed that the truth of the old adage would receive a further confirmation in the case of the "Andromeda." Her captain at least thought so, as a sailor hastily approached him with the information that the vessel was making water fast.

Attempts were immediately made to discover the cause, but without avail, and the men were then ordered to the pumps. Frank could not remain idle where help was required, and he therefore took his turn with the others, cheering them on with encouraging words, and more by the calm unconcern with which he regarded the surrounding danger. A certain future had deprived him, as it will all those who ensure it, of that cowardly, cringing fear with which men regard the ills and vicissitudes of life.

"Vee must save zee ship mit all hazards !" exclaimed the captain, approaching Frank. "I have never lost von ship yet, und ven it is mine fault I vill not lose zee 'Andromeda.'"

"About ship !" he called out to the steersman.

"Vee must, however, prepare for all emergencies," he added, and turning to the first mate, he said : "See dat zee boats is made ready mit provisions und mit every ting necessary."

"Ven vee are lucky und can keep zee ship afloat mit three days, vee can reach an Island off zee coast of South America, vere vee can put zee "Andromeda" to rights, at least sufficiently to enable us to reach zee mainland."

The united efforts of the men were, however, unable to prevent the water from gaining upon them, and the conviction that their fate was sealed caused some dissension amongst the crew, who were anxious to be relieved from what they considered useless labour. Day and night they worked on unceasingly, and the storm continued to rage in the bosom of the ocean, and to rend the heavens with its threatening thunders and its flashes of forked and vivid light. At the close of the second day a change for the better occurred.

The gale which had been blowing died away in soft and gentle zephyrs, which seemed to Frank like the sweet cadences in a wild harmony, touching the hidden springs of a longed-for joy, and awakening the soul from strained and awful conceptions to the gentler influences of love.

The carpenter, who had been busily occupied in looking for the leak which had caused the crew so much anxiety, at last succeeded in discovering and stopping it.

In her disabled condition, however, the captain deemed it right not to alter the course of the "Andromeda." "but," said he to Frank, "if zee vetter (weather)

becomes goot, I tink vee vill perhaps make for Rio
Janeiro to-morrow. Vee can reach it mit two days fon
now mit fair vetter—den you can take zee first ship to
England und be home mit no time. Den dese vaga-
bonds vill smart, und mine thoughts vill come true,
and—ach, vell, dat lovely girl May vill be yours!"

"How do you know that?" said Frank, upon whom
the merest reference to his darling May acted like the
breeze which blows from the face of the sun the cloud
which hides from view its warm genial beams.

"Potztausend—dat goes mitout mine saying—vell, vell,
I hopes to have zee pleasure von day of seeing you both
mit zee same name. Ach! von bright idea has just
struck me mit von force dat——" and here the captain
laughed and turned away from Frank, rubbing his hands
and exulting like a man who has just discovered a gold
mine, and needs but to turn the sod to reap a golden
harvest of wealth.

"Whatever is the matter with the fellow?" said Frank,
looking at the captain with an air of amusement. "Out
with it, captain; you will choke yourself if you go on in
that way."

"Vell, vell," replied the captain, "it is not very much
after all. You say I tink in England dat zee English-
man's house is his castle. Vell, ven you get von house

I vill make you von suggestion. May vill be its Queen, und it vill be your citadel—call it 'Mayville.'"

"Not so bad for you, captain—just to strain a point, we'll say its a good example of verbicide."

With pleasant banter of this kind the day soon passed, and the morrow found them safe in Rio Janeiro.

CHAPTER VII.

AT the time at which the events herein narrated occurred, there were in close proximity to the Liverpool Docks many narrow lanes and alleys in which vast numbers of our river people were congregated.

In one of these, not far from the Landing-stage, and near to St. Paul's Church, might be seen an old tumble-down cottage, of the type characteristic of narrow, stuffy courts, in which even the houses seem to suffer from the want of pure air and sunshine.

Leaning slightly forward, and coated with dirty white-wash to about half its height, the cottage looked any-thing but a desirable abode. And yet there was a jaunty, rollicking air about the old place, which har-monized with its inhabitants, and acted in some degree as a charm upon them.

In the small room at the back of the house a man and a youth were seated at a deal table, engaged in earnest conversation.

"But, father, are you sure he was drowned?" asked the youth, who, to judge from appearances, was evidently what is termed, in vulgar parlance, a "sharper."

"Sartin," gruffly responded the man thus addressed. "As soon as I got on top of the old boat, I looked round for my pals and the young cove, but they was gone. Not a cry nor nothing could I hear, until I heard yer calling out cheery-like from the 'Saucy Poll,' and caught the line you hove. Yer see I was," he said apologetically, "in such a state I scarcely knew anything. Arter all it's well them er pals is out o' the way; they can't tell no tales, and then the coin won't have to be bunced. Poll, Poll," he called to his wife, who was preparing supper in the kitchen, "heap on some more coal, and fetch in summut stronger 'n water."

"I suppose," continued the youth, "when you received the £100 for the job, you did not tell them how it had been performed?"

"Not one word; do yer think I'd be such a flat as to spoil our chance of more tin? No, no," replied the man, in whom we have all no doubt recognised Jerry Mills.

"No," he proceeded, "I jist said the job's done neatly, and yer'l hear no more on't, take my davy if yer will."

"But," said young Mills, "did they not make any inquiries?"

"No," replied Jerry. "I s'pose they thought as how as ignorance war wisdom, or some sich proverb as that."

"Never mind quotations, father," said young Mills, laughingly, "what about our plans for the future? We must be exceedingly careful how we proceed!"

"Jest so—careful how we perceed," reiterated Jerry, musingly, from the centre of a small cloud of tobacco-smoke in which he had enveloped himself.

"What's a hundred," he continued, "for a job o' this sort? We must have a thou' or two afore we're shaken off."

"I rather grumbled like, arter I got the cash from young Dove, jest ter let him know that he war in my power, and that he might look forrard to another visit o' the same kind from yours trooly. I jest let him know he'd better have some cash handy next time I called."

"Well, and what did he say?" asked Mills, junior.

"He looked more'n he said—and then 'sulted with the old chap, who fired up like, and said as how the bisness war done, and I might go."

"You see," said young Mills, "you are, to a certain extent, bound to keep silence for your own safety, and no doubt these Doves (a pretty name for such creatures) know that as well as we do."

"True," said Jerry, "but yer see I have some strangely-worded letters and telegrams from them parties, which, if a third party got hold on—you for instance—could with ease frighten them out o' their wits and cash. Yer could say in a note, and yer knows well how to write one better nor me, how as a friend o' yourn, Jerry Mills by name, was taken suddenly ill, and that afore he died he confessed the whole bisness, told yer how as yer could produce evidence, living evidence, and then gave yer dokyments."

"Splendid," said young Mills, "that plan did not occur to me."

"But," continued Jerry, "I don't want to die, threti-cally, I thinks yer call it, jest yet; I am jest agoin to annoy them Doves a little.

"Yer see they has a fine office, and a number o' young gents employed, and it would never do to be having a handsome cove like me a hanging round too often; some cove might smell a rat, seeing what happened o' late."

"What has happened? You never mentioned anything to me. I don't know what you mean," said young Mills.

"Jest give a cove time," said Jerry. "Yer knows I went down to Manchester the other day, jest to look round a little and see if I could pick up any news as would prove handy, when who should I meet but Tom Bunkus!"

"Tom Bunkus; let me see," interrupted Mills, junior, "is that the man who owned the 'Pretty Jane' down here?"

"The same," continued Jerry. "Well, yer see, he's now the owner o' a neat little pub., near the Manchester Exchange.

"Says he to me, slapping me on the shoulder, hearty like, 'Jerry, old pal, what brings yer down to Manchester?' 'Jest havin' a bit o' a holiday,' I says. 'Well then,' says he, 'come into my little bit o' property and have something as'll warm yer.' O' course I did not refuse the invitation, and we were soon comfortable like in his snug. Well, we got talking about one thing and another, as had happened since we met afore. 'Tom,' says I, 'there's many ups and downs in this life.' 'True for you, old pal,' he says, 'but I've nought to complain on, seeing as I've had more ups nor downs!' We were looking out o' the window when he said this, and who should pass hurriedly, but Mr. Dove.

"'That's a fortunate man,' says Tom, pointing old Dove out, with a nod o' his head. 'Is he,' says I, not letting on as I knew him, but at the same time thinking that he was rather unfortunate at being in the power o' that honest, soft-hearted individil, Jerry Mills.

"'What's happened to him, Tom?' says I, hoping to get something as would be useful.

"'Come in fur a lot o' money,' says Tom. 'Has he?' says I; 'tell us all about it, Tom.'

"'Well,' says he, 'to make a long story short, there was an old fellow here the other day as lives at Crompton, and in the course o' conversation, we spoke about fortune, jest incidental like, as we have to-day.

"'Whilst we were discussin' the subject, Mr. Dove, who has an office in this neighbourhood, jest dropped in fur a sup o' brandy, and arter he left the old chap told me that some relative o' Dove's, named Mrs. Walton, had died, and as he was the nearest relative living, and there was no Will, he came in fur the property—a very heavy sum, I believe.

"'But, with all his cash, he hasn't a morsel o' charity, the mean skunk,' says Tom. 'It's always the case with

these fellows who come in for cash suddenly; their
greedy appetites are never satisfied no how!'

"Thinks I, that's one to you, Jerry, but I says nothing,
and he perceeded:

"'One would think that when Fortune smiles on a
man his heart would expand, and his hand open to the
poor and needy.'

"'Why, Tom,' I says, 'yer quite a preacher, which,
to say the least, is rather a new thing in your purfes-
sion. I 'spose yer follers yer own max—what do yer
call—ims?'

"'Jerry,' says he, quite solemnly, placing his hand on
my shoulder, 'it's not for a man to blow his own
trumpet, but this I says, that never a poor body has
sought my help in vain since I've had a bit to spare.

"'Do yer think because a man's a publican that
every grain o' sympathy and humanity is crushed out o'
his nature?'

"And he looked at me so fiercely as he said this, that
I thought I must say something as would tone him
down a little, so I says, 'Not at all, Tom; not at all.
Yer always was good hearted, Tom, and a pub's not
sich a bad affair arter all.'

"'But, Jerry, I'm a goin' to get out o' it as soon as
possible—it's not that I do any harm, fur,' says he, 'I

never sarved a man as had had enough as was good
fur him yet, but it's the sights one sees—people will
abuse it.'

· "'They will,' says I, not caring much for this kind o'
talk, as it made me feel slightly oncomfortable in view
o' the things as has happened o' late, so I says, kind
o' mildly: 'This is nice rum o' yourn, Tom, werry nice
rum; I don't mind if I try jest a thimbleful more.'

"'That's jest it,' he says, 'all the world over—acquire
a taste, and then yer've got to find the means o' gratifying it.'

"'Quite true,' I says, 'but yer never told me why yer
called that cove as passed here stingy,' fearing that with
all his palaver he'd miss givin' me the 'ticklers.

"'I'm ashamed to talk o' it,' he says. 'What did old
Dove do first thing arter he got the cash but turn into
the street an old woman named Betsy, as was a faithful
servant to the party as died, fur many a long year, and
as nursed her in her long illness.'

"'Out upon him,' he says, stamping his foot upon the
ground, 'I believe as how as I could hang a fellow like
him. And then,' he went on to say, 'there's something curious in the story, as Betsy seems to think the
cash should have gone to a nevvy, named Frank Amer-
ton, or Atherton.'

"When he said this, I gave sich a start as made him look at me rather curiously. 'What's the matter, Jerry?' says he. 'Only a pain in my stomach,' I says. 'P'raps a drop more o' that rum o' yourn would put me to rights.' Arter this we changed the topic, and in a short time I shook hands with him and left."

"You got some valuable information, and I imagine now that I will be the best to follow up the clue," said young Mills.

"What do yer propose?" said Jerry.

"I will go down to Crompton, find out this old Betsy, and get all particulars out of her. There can, however, be no doubt that, even with the information we now possess, we have a firm hold on the Doves, and as we could do with some more cash now, you had better pay your contemplated visit to-morrow."

CHAPTER VIII.

OME five months have now elapsed since the disappearance of Frank, and his friends have by this time, it may be thought, given up all hope of discovering anything tangible respecting his fate.

It is true that there were many suppositions rife which pretended to account for his singular disparition, but each as it was presented to the little circle from which Frank's absence was most keenly felt, was scouted as being, if not utterly beyond the bounds of possibility, at least outside the pale with which an ever-lingering hope had bounded their imaginations.

They would persist in recalling instances of a like nature about which they had read, and which tended to foster the hope they were so loathe to resign.

In this it cannot, we think, be urged that they formed any exception to the general rule; and whilst

we are ready to admit that there are those who ever
look to the dark and shady side of nature, yet we
believe the majority of our race cling to hope—bright,
fair, cheerful hope—with the tenacity with which a
drowning man grasps a straw, not even relaxing the
hold with death itself. How often has the remark,
"We cannot realize it," been passed by those between
whom and some loved one the dark river of death has
suddenly flowed; and in this feeling may we not recognise
the last struggle to retain what we know to be a
fleeting, vain, delusive hope.

And whilst the character of Hope herself is not free
from sable stains, can we wonder that Frank's friends
at times lost sight of her cheery face, and saw but the
dark mantle which protected her from the keen blasts
of fear ?

Often May would weep when alone in her chamber,
weep hot scalding tears, which one might readily conjecture would obliterate from her memory the many
scenes which her imagination had conjured up respecting
her friendship, perhaps future alliance, with Frank. But
Memory was faithful, and would persist in bringing hope
back to May's assistance whenever she was thus tempted
to give way to grief.

As respects the Doves, they had already begun to feel

keenly the annoyance and anxiety which the now frequent visits of Jerry Mills caused them, but they consoled themselves in the thought that they would soon be beyond the sea, and the power of Jerry.

In this, however, they were to be mistaken—they had yet to learn the truth of the proverb, "Man proposes, God disposes."

Their knowledge of human affairs was limited by an experience in which but material matters formed the whole, and their bad motives precluded all idea of a wise and loving God ruling the universe, and ordering and disposing all things in accordance with His gracious will and purpose.

Jerry Mills and his son, as will have been seen from the foregoing, had not been idle, but, by continual visits and threatenings, had succeeding in extorting from the Doves £500 in excess of the amount for which their nefarious bargain had been entered into. Further than this, the visit of young Mills to Crompton had proved most unfortunate for the schemes of the Doves, inasmuch as the fact that they contemplated removing their residence had by this means become known. It seems that after visiting Betsy, Will Mills had, out of curiosity, spent an hour or two in the neighbourhood of the villa occupied by Mr. Dove. Here he observed that arrange-

ments were being made for the removal of the furniture,
and conjectured that the Doves intended to take refuge
from his father's hands in flight. This seemed all the
more probable, when he considered the statement Betsy
had made to him as to the fortune left by Mrs.
Walton. "Old Dove," he muttered, "has now plenty
of cash; and as from what my father gathered, he was
much in debt before he came in for it, I imagine he
will rid himself of the debts and my father by 'clearing;'
but I'll stop him—he will not shake me off as easily
as his creditors."

Whilst he was thus engaged in discussing the question
with himself, he noticed that a van had been drawn
up at the back entrance to Mr. Dove's mansion, and
he determined to watch closely, in order that he might
find out the destination of the furniture, and, if possible,
the true motive for this, to him, suspicious procedure
on the part of Mr. Dove.

After the van had been loaded it moved slowly away
in the direction of the railway station, and another
approached and commenced loading.

Mills followed the first van to the station, where he
entered into conversation with the driver, and by the
aid of an "allowance" succeeded in getting out of him
the fact that the furniture was going to a certain

auctioneer's rooms in London. He then telegraphed the
particulars to his father, in phraseology which no stranger
could understand, and advised him to at once proceed
to London (indicating the address), and to be ready
for all emergencies. What he exactly meant by this
concluding piece of advice it is difficult for us to premise;
but we think we are not far wrong when, judging from
our knowledge of the desperate character of Jerry, we
state that he would not have any scruples which would
prevent him from taking from him, his enemy, that
beyond which all human revenge is powerless to proceed.

Jerry, as soon as he received the message, set about
carrying out its injunction; and scarcely eight hours had
elapsed before he arrived in London, had secured an apartment in a boarding house which faced the rooms of the
auctioneer to whom Mr. Dove's furniture was consigned
and was vigilantly watching for something to occur
which would throw a light upon this intrigue. The
night came on, however, without bringing with it anything but dark and threatening clouds; and Jerry, as he
looked upon the sky from the window of his room,
could scarcely repress a shudder, as it reminded him of
the night upon which he had attempted the life of
our hero, and upon which he had so nearly lost his
own.

Whilst these thoughts were occupying his mind, a sudden flash of lightning illumined the street, and there, on the opposite side, he beheld Frank Atherton.

With a cry of alarm he stepped back from the window, and placed his hands over his eyes, to shut out what he believed to be a horrid, ill-foreboding vision. But all to no purpose—nothing could obliterate the sight of that pale face. He could see it looking at him which ever way he turned and the guilty wretch fairly trembled and groaned at the thoughts which this sudden vision had aroused.

Jerry was an exceedingly ignorant man, and, like most of that description of humanity, he was also very superstitious. He had heard of such things as the spirits of dead men haunting those who had done them evil, and wreaking upon them a terrible vengeance, and as these stories crowded in upon his mind he became perfectly terrified. He had sown corruption, and the day of reaping was at hand! He had stained his life with crimes and acts of inhumanity, and now his deeds were to receive the punishment they merited!!

Who can estimate the agony of mind that Jerry suffered that night with that pale, reproachful face looking into his very soul, and the feeling which oppressed him and forced the dire conviction upon him, that some fearful doom was impending which would ere long crush him out of existence.

But Jerry had seen no vision! The day he had arrived in London proved singularly to be the one upon which Frank, for the first time since his strange adventure, placed his foot upon his native soil. He had come to London from Rio Janeiro by means of a small sailing vessel which belonged to that port, and at the time Jerry caught sight of him he was returning to his hotel from St. Pancras Station, to which he had been to see his solicitor off to Liverpool by the night express.

Frank had landed towards the close of the day, and had gone at once to see Mr. Agile, a solicitor with whom he had formerly been acquainted. Of course Frank discussed his affairs with him, and as the matter was one which did not admit of any delay, Mr. Agile determined to proceed that night to Liverpool.

He intended to break the news of Frank's return to Mr. Atherton, and then, with his assistance, endeavour to connect the links in the chain of evidence which had been outlined to him.

Of course Frank had not heard of his father's illness, and no doubt his ignorance of the fact saved him from much pain and anxiety.

G

Captain Winklestein, with whom Frank had parted at Rio Janeiro, had, after effecting the needful repairs to the "Andromeda," proceeded on his journey, having, however, first wished Frank every success in unravelling the mystery which had resulted in their acquaintanceship, and promised that when he next returned to Liverpool, at the following Christmas he hoped, he would not fail to pay Frank a visit. "Perhaps," he said, with a sly look, as he lingered on the quay, "it vill not only be Master Frank, but also zee sweet May mit Frank's name. Potztausend! but you vill be von lucky boy. I vish I vas in your boots den."

Frank could not help feeling pleased at the allusion to his little *douce amie*, although he told the captain it was too bad of him to be always treating him to "chaff."

If we had said otherwise of Frank it would, we consider, have been tantamount to a declaration that he was not human, for what man, although he may not care to make an exhibition of his feelings, does not experience a sensation of pride at being associated with beauty, particularly so when such beauty takes the form of a loving, gentle girl?

The mere mention of her name is sufficient to open wide the barrier which momentarily excludes him from an elysium of bright, enchanting visions.

A morning or two after Frank's arrival, he was walking leisurely about the city, thinking over his affairs, and wondering why he had received no communication from his solicitor, when his attention was arrested by a number of people entering an auctioneer's rooms. Seeing the announcement of a large sale of furniture, &c., and thinking that this would afford him perhaps a little recreation and relaxation from the harassing thoughts which possessed his mind, he entered, and for a time, thanks to the pleasant banter of the auctioneer, he certainly became oblivious to everything but that which was passing around him.

Ere long, however, something in the style of the furniture reminded him very much of that which his aunt had; and he might have been heard muttering, "Surely nothing has happened to her; I could almost swear to that old cabinet. I'll make a bid for it for the sake of old associations. It may come in, too," he thought, as a glimpse of the "Mayville," Captain Winkelstein had pictured to him, presented itself to his mental vision. "It may; it may," he muttered audibly, with an affectionate lingering on the last utterance.

The sale proceeded, and before Frank had time to realise what he was about he had purchased almost all the articles which bore some resemblance to those which belonged to his relative. In the excitement of the moment he forgot that he was almost destitute of cash, and would be so until he received the promised communication from his solicitor. However, he deposited what money he had in his possession with the auctioneer, the latter expressing himself satisfied on receiving a promise that the balance would be paid within a week.

On examining the cabinet, in an ante-room, where he was removed from the gaze of the busy traffickers, he was soon convinced that it was the identical one which had stood in his aunt's room; and remembering what she had once told him, when quite a little fellow, about its secret drawer, he opened it, discovered and pressed the spring, and before him lay his aunt's Bible. Eagerly he seized it, and unclasped its covers, and, as he did so, a document fell from within fluttering to his feet.

Hastily he picked it up, noticing, as he did so, the words "Last Will and Testament," and without allowing himself time to read further, he put it into his pocket, restored the Bible to its place, and walked off rapidly to his hotel.

As he turned the corner of the street he almost stumbled upon the Doves, who had just arrived in the City and who were approaching, arm in arm, from the opposite direction, but his mind was so preoccupied that he did not notice them.

They, however, started, drew back, and then precipitately entered an hotel. Here they held a whispered consultation, after assuring themselves that they had not been seen, and decided to quit the country without delay.

The other members of Mr. Dove's family had gone on the Continent some few weeks previously, and there was, therefore, nothing to hamper the movements of the two men.

They would first call upon the auctioneer, get from him what money he could advance, and then take the train for Dover.

Following out this plan, they proceeded to the auctioneer's rooms, received from him a portion of the money due to them, called a cab, and drove off to the railway station.

Meanwhile Jerry Mills had been joined by his son, and having seen the Doves enter the house opposite in an excited state, and guessing that some important move was now to be made, they prepared to follow and, at all hazards, to prevent the Doves from quitting the country, at least without leaving behind them a large portion of the money acquired through their instrumentality.

Quickly calling a cab, they instructed the driver to follow that which was rapidly conveying the Doves to their destination.

CHAPTER IX.

"A love so violent, so strong, so sure,
That neither age can change, nor art can cure."

"AH me! Words could not more truly picture my case. If I could only forget him—ah, if—but I cannot. His very words, his looks, his manner seem engraven on my heart. Even Time, that fell destroyer, I fear will fail to erase the slightest of the impressions which he has made upon me. But, why should I fear? I do not desire that these sweet recollections and feelings should fade and become things of the past, and that this fountain, which is the source of many joys, should be sealed. Oh, no! It is but the thought that he who created them may never meet these eyes again, may never know the wealth of love my fond heart would lavish upon him, which gives me sorrow. I am sure he loved me, for his eyes revealed the secret which his lips refused to tell. This bitter separation, his uncertain fate—these are the sable springs from which my troubles flow."

And the speaker moved up and down a narrow avenue in the garden which surrounded her home, an avenue which lavish nature had adorned with varied beauties. As one gazed upon its ivy-clad sides, and then upon the gentle maiden who walked between them, no human power could prevent the thought that this beautiful ivy was a fitting emblem of her constancy, a living type of a tender nature which clings tenaciously to another, and draws from it life and refreshment.

Raising her head, with eyes bedewed with tears, she gave vent to her pent-up feelings in song. Softly the words:

'When the wild swans wander home,
 'Where the fragrant citrons bloom,
'When the sun thro' forest green
 'Bids farewell to day's bright scene.
'Then my heart—my throbbing heart,
 'Fondly sighs as these depart,
'Wilt thou, too, return again?
 'Parting, ah! parting is bitter pain.

'Lonely heart why thus opprest?
 'Thou 'ere long shalt find thy rest;
'Tho' from earth all fade away,
 'Soon will dawn a brighter day.

'Then, poor heart, poor faithful heart,
  'Trustful say 'ere all depart;
'Soon shall I meet thee again
  'Where is no more parting nor pain.'

floated upwards, until they mingled with the joyous notes of the feathered songsters, and died away in a long, sweet cadency.

A tinge of sadness sometimes adds to rather than deprives of beauty the face it invades—the subdued light of the eye, the relaxation of features perhaps too sharply defined, occasionally intensify beauty, and render its charms more alluring.

This was eminently so in the case of our songstress, who was none other than May Jeffries, the dear girl upon whom our hero had set his heart.

As she turned out of the avenue she observed a stranger open the garden gate and walk towards the house; and as he had the appearance of a legal gentleman, May, fairly trembling in the anticipation of news respecting Frank, bounded round to the side entrance of the house, and was in readiness to receive the stranger when he arrived.

"Is Mr. Jeffries at home?" he enquired of the maid who responded to his summons.

"Yes," she replied, and as she showed him into the drawing-room, said, "Who shall I say wishes to see him?"

"Mr. Agile, solicitor, London. Kindly say that my business is pressing."

May, who had heard all that had passed from the breakfast room, at once hurried off to her father and Mr. Atherton, who were enjoying a morning paper in the library.

Mr. Atherton, it must here be stated, had now, owing to the kindly treatment he had received, almost quite recovered from the illness which had been brought on by the loss of his son, and was contemplating a speedy return to business.

"Come, papa, at once," said May, springing into the room, "a gentleman from London wishes to see you on important business."

"His name?" demanded the Squire.

"Mr. Agile, solicitor, London."

As May uttered the name Mr. Atherton started, and said rapidly "Frank had some acquaintance of that name; he must bring some news."

"If that is the case, one would imagine that he does. At all events, I don't know anybody of that name myself. We'll go to him at once," said the Squire.

On entering the drawing-room, Mr. Agile rose to meet the Squire, stating, as he did so, that he had been informed that a Mr. Atherton, of Liverpool, was at present staying with him.

"Will you have the goodness, then, to ask him to be present during our interview. I bring news respecting his absent son which will prove both welcome and gladdening."

"Thank God! he lives! he lives!" ejaculated the Squire, and hurried off to bring Mr. Atherton and May to hear the lawyer's story.

The old Squire's joyful countenance and excited manner revealed his secret to the occupants of the library before he could give it utterance, and the ejaculation which fell from his lips was repeated in glad tones by the anxious parent and the loving girl.

Quickly they repaired to the drawing-room, and without delay Mr. Agile told the story of Frank's adventures, and of his safe return to England. How eagerly they listened to the particulars, and May, as she heard of the disaster on the Mersey, exchanged a significant glance with her father.

It reminded her of her dream, and she shuddered to think how nearly it had been fulfilled.

"But," said Mr. Atherton, "we should have learned some of these details from the 'Andromeda's' pilot."

"True, but there was no pilot on board," rejoined Mr. Agile. "For some reason, best known to himself, he did not put in an appearance, and the vessel, therefore sailed without him."

After he had finished his recital, Mr. Agile said, "I have one thing to enjoin for the present, and that is, that not a word be breathed of Frank's return." It is necessary, if I am to succeed in finding out the per· petrators, and the reason of the outrage committed upon my friend, that everything should be done *sub rosa.*"

"But how do you propose to proceed?" asked Squire Jeffries.

"I purpose first to visit Mrs. Walton, and ——."

"Mrs. Walton"—they cried out in a breath—"is dead."

"Oh! When did she die?"

"Shorty after the disappearance of Frank," replied the Squire.

"Ah! and who has come into the possession of her property?" continued Mr. Agile.

"Mr. Dove, a relative of hers," responded Mr. Atherton.

"Frank, I think, told me that a Mr. Dove had a house in this neighbourhood; is that so?" said Mr. Agile.

"It is," responded the Squire, "but my servant told me the other morning that some of the furniture was being taken to the railway station, and I therefore fancy he must contemplate removing."

"I must now wish you good day," said Mr. Agile, rather abruptly, "you will readily, I think, understand the necessity of immediate action on my part."

"Have a little luncheon first," said the Squire, "May, just ——."

"No, thanks; another time," said Mr. Agile, smiling pleasantly, and taking up his hat, "my nature, I feel this moment is bent upon proving its right to the name I bear."

"Well, then, accept our best thanks for the welcome news you have brought us, and tell Frank how happy you have made us by imparting the knowledge of his safety. I suppose we may not write to him just yet?" said the Squire.

"No; I think it would not be prudent to do so. Bye the bye, I had almost forgotten," he said, addressing Mr. Atherton, "to give you a note which Frank entrusted me with."

Mr. Atherton tore the communication open as he recognized the handwriting of his boy; and after glancing through its contents, he left the room for a moment, and returned with a small package, which he handed to Frank's solicitor.

"Thanks," said the latter, "I will take care that you are informed of all that transpires, and now I must wish you good day."

After quitting Squire Jeffries' residence, Mr. Agile walked on to the railway station, resolving as he went upon the line of action he would take. "I must find out first," he said to himself, "the destination of the furniture, and then I will go on to Manchester, and try to learn something more about this Mr. Dove. It seems to me that I am on the right track."

On reaching the railway station he soon obtained the particulars he required respecting the furniture, and then, following out the programme he had arranged, he took the first train to Manchester.

His task was certainly no easy one now. In the heart of a strange, busy city, information was not so readily obtainable respecting individuals as at Crompton, and before the day closed Mr. Agile, tired and worn out, became painfully aware of the fact.

He had promised to write to Frank each day during his absence from the Metropolis, but on entering the hotel at which he had decided to pass the night, he was so overcome with fatigue, that he was compelled to retire without fulfilling his engagement.

The next morning he rose refreshed, and, after breakfasting, he wrote to Frank, giving all particulars, and enclosing the package from Mr. Atherton. The note he sent under cover to his head clerk, who had received instructions as to its disposal.

The note despatched in time for the early train, he

took up a directory, ascertained the names of the owners of the various restaurants, hotels, and public-houses in the immediate neighbourhood of Mr. Dove's office, and subsequently quitted the hotel for the purpose of prosecuting his enquiries.

At about ten o'clock in the morning he found himself in the public-house owned by Mr. Thomas Bunkus, and having ordered some luncheon, he entered into conversation with the individual mentioned.

Mr. Bunkus's favourite topic was, as we have previously discerned, fortune.

He had, for a man of his class, amassed a considerable sum of money, and his heart was so filled with the importance of the fact that he could not abstain from talking about it.

Mr. Agile, therefore, with the facility with which men of his profession become possessed of information, soon had drawn from Mr. Bunkus all he knew respecting the Doves.

"He generally passes here about this time," said Bunkus, and if you like I'll point him out to you."

"Thanks; I should like to see such a fortunate man very much," said Mr. Agile, "although," he added, "I do not base my estimate of men upon the quantity of filthy lucre they may possess!"

"Then upon what do you base it?" asked Bunkus, opening his eyes rather wider than was good for them.

"Upon their actions principally," replied Mr. Agile; "but," he added, "do not imagine that I despise wealth; on the contrary, I think it has its mission. What I do hate, however, is this constant devotion at the altar of the golden calf, and forgetfulness of the Giver of all good.

"That is Mr. Dove and his son passing now," said Mr. Bunkus, pointing them out.

"Indeed; well, good day, Mr. Bunkus, I must be off," said Mr. Agile, hastily leaving the room with the intention of following the Doves.

When in the street he observed, at a short distance in the rear of Mr. Dove, a youth of sailor-like appearance, who, so it seemed to Mr. Agile, was watching narrowly, and with something more than curiosity, the movements of the cotton merchant.

"The case becomes interesting," thought Mr. Agile, and he determined, if possible, to keep an eye on the trio.

It soon became apparent, from the direction they took, that the Doves were bent upon leaving the city.

Becoming bolder as he reached the railway station, our friend rapidly neared the Doves, in order that he might learn the name of the place for which they took tickets, but he was foiled in this by the intervention of young Mills, for it was he whom Mr. Agile had previously noticed following Mr. Dove.

Mills, of course, had the same object in view as Mr. Agile, but being made of rougher material than the latter, he was not so particular as to whom he inconvenienced in the attainment of it. He was not known to either of the Doves, and, therefore, he had nothing to fear in a crowded railway station, at least, so he thought.

"That young fellow is certainly intent upon his business," said Mr. Agile, rather chagrined at being jostled and defeated in his design by Mills, "however, I will wait and see what train they enter. It seems strange and suspicious to me that a seafaring man should be following these merchants about; and, as Frank was assaulted by some of his class, there seems to be some truth in what that German captain premised. I wish I had a detective or two with me."

At this moment the London train drew up at the platform, and seeing Mr. Dove advance towards it, Mr. Agile, quickly obtained a ticket, and soon the party were speeding on towards the great Metropolis, the one-half exulting in the seeming success of their plans, and the other plotting how best to defeat them.

CHAPTER X.

FRANK, shortly after returning to his hotel, received the note sent to him by his solicitor; and after perusing its contents, he decided to communicate at once with Mr. Agile, and advise him to place the matter without further delay in the hands of the police. This would perhaps have been the most natural course to have pursued in the first instance, but the dread of hindering his cause by acting too precipitately, had restrained Frank from doing so.

He had thought that the better mode of procedure would be to leave the matter entirely in the hands of his friend, in whose discrimination and discretion he had unlimited confidence.

It was with no small amount of satisfaction that he learned the particulars of the lawyer's reception at Squire Jeffries', but the news of the death of Mrs.

II

Walton filled him with sad and painful feelings. He had anticipated the fact the moment her Will came into his possession, and it was this primarily which made him seek the solitude of his chamber in such haste.

"Poor aunt," he said, "how she loved me! The uncertainty of my lot must have acted detrimentally upon her health. I wish I had been present to comfort her in her last moments; it would have at least been some source of solace to me now. But Fate willed it otherwise. It reminds me of that ill-foreboding dream I had on my return passage. Ah! here are the verses I wrote on waking :—

> ' The night enclosed in sable hue
> 'Fair Nature's form and face,
> ' Till all her charms were hid from view,
> 'In that abhorred embrace.
> 'No moon, no stars, to cheer my way,
> ' Their light thro' air distilled,
> ' No gladdening sounds, to my dismay,
> ' The ruling hush dispelled.
>
> 'Methought that never more would shine
> 'The sun's kind genial ray,
> ' That light would ne'er again define
> ' The beauties of the day ;
> ' That all things fair, and bright, and dear
> ' To earth had bid adieu,
> 'And ne'er would come again to cheer,
> ' Or pleasures past renew.'

"I wonder," he said, on reading them, "whether I shall ever be able to pen the antithesis? It ought to be so," he continued, meditatively; "heaven has been kind to me this morning. How remarkable it is that I should come into the possession of my aunt's Will and furniture. I have now at least the means of wresting from the Doves the remains of my aunt's fortune, if I should be unsuccessful in bringing home to them the crime of attempting my life."

Frank little thought that at the very moment he made this remark, his enemies were fleeing away, taking with them the fortune which belonged to him.

Mr. Dove, the elder, who at first had shewn some pretensions to the possession of a conscience, had long since placed a veto upon its warning and convicting voice, and he had determined to go to almost any length to render certain the success of all his plans. He certainly felt somewhat relieved that Jerry had not taken Frank's life, but, at the same time, his and his son's anxiety to leave the shores of England with their ill-gotten gains was greatly increased.

What if their fraud should be discovered? What if they should be intercepted in their flight, and handed over to the tender mercies of the law? These were questions which troubled the Doves, and gave them wings with which to increase the rapidity of their flight.

They would endeavour to quieten each other's fears by saying that it was utterly impossible for anything to be discovered. Had they not left their manager under the impression that they were going out of town for a few days only, and given him full instructions to ensure the proper conduct of business during their absence. This would allay all suspicion of the impending surprise at Manchester; and had not the sale of the furniture been carried out in a most successful and quiet manner. It was ridiculous to imagine that any circumstance could now arise which would deprive them of both wealth and liberty. So they tried to think, but their guilt refused to admit of the sense of safety which their arguments would fain have induced.

Mr. Agile, on arriving in London, took a cab and drove to the hotel at which Frank was staying. He did not wait to be announced, but rushed into the room in which our hero was, surprising the latter in the midst of some gloomy reflections.

"You here, Mr. Agile!" he ejaculated, and advanced to meet him. "What has brought you back so soon, and in such a state of excitement? You surely have not already discovered the villain?"

"What is this?" said Mr. Agile, not heeding the question, as his practised eye caught sight of the legal document on the table.

"My aunt's Will," replied Frank. "I found it quite by ——."

"Never mind telling me the particulars now," said Mr. Agile, "there is not a moment to spare. Let me see," he continued, glancing through the Will rapidly, "she leaves you by this all her possessions, with the exception of a small annuity to a domestic. This is fortunate. Quick, Mr. Atherton—your hat—follow me," he sputtered out as he quitted the room in the hasty manner in which he had entered it. Frank followed, wondering what was going to happen, jumped into the cab in which he found his solicitor waiting, and heard with something akin to astonishment the instructions to the driver.

"I purposed writing when you disturbed me, to advise you to procure the assistance of the detective force, but you seem to have quite anticipated me in this."

"Yes; it has become necessary. Mr. Dove and his son are in London, and if I mistake not, will quit it and England for ever within a few hours from now. We have, therefore, not a moment to lose if we are to be successful in preventing their escape."

He then told Frank, as they drove to Scotland Yard, all that had transpired since he had written to him, with the result that Frank was more than ever certain that the Doves were the authors of all his misery

Mr. Agile was well known at the Detective office, and in a short time he had secured the services of four strong men, and had obtained the documents necessary to enable them to arrest the Doves.

"Now for the auctioneer's rooms, where I think we shall secure our men," said Mr. Agile, as they re-entered their conveyance, after obtaining another for the Detectives.

"If the Doves are where we suppose, we will not make the arrest immediately," he continued, after a short pause, during which he had been turning the matter over in his mind. "If I mistake not, we shall, by the exercise of a little caution, find one or more of the dastardly fellows who perpetrated the outrage upon you. I am convinced the young fellow I saw following the Doves had something to do with the affair."

"Will you be able to identify the scoundrels, Mr. Atherton?" he asked.

"The one with whom I had the greatest struggle," replied Frank, "but not the others."

The conveyances were stopped a short distance from the auctioneer's place of business; and Mr. Agile, after cautioning Frank not to show himself for the present, alighted and walked past the bureau alluded to, scrutinizing the occupants carefully as he did so.

Seeing that Mr. Dove was not there, he entered, with the view of eliciting some information from the auctioneer. The latter, however, could give no definite replies to Mr. Agile's queries. He thought Mr. Dove intended going on the Continent for a few weeks, but he did not know positively.

"My business is of a very urgent nature," said Mr. Agile. "I suppose you do not expect to see Mr. Dove again to-day?" "No, I do not; but the cabman who drove him away from here is just passing, no doubt he can tell you to where he drove Mr. Dove," said the auctioneer. "Thanks," said Mr. Agile "I will ask him," and turning into the street he hailed the cabman, and on making his enquiry, learned that the gentlemen who had been "picked up" at the auctioneer's had been driven to Charing Cross station.

Taking out his watch, he saw that he would be unable to catch the Dover train leaving Charing Cross at 6.15 p.m. What should he do? Here was a dilemma. All at once it occurred to him that a train left Cannon Street station some ten or fifteen minutes later, and without losing any further time, Mr. Agile, Frank, and escort drove off to the last-mentioned place.

"Most unfortunate," said Mr. Agile, "he may now escape us—that is unless that sailor-fellow prevents him."

"I rather fancy he had some such purpose in view."

"But," said Frank, "if he is whom we imagine, he could have no other object but the squeezing of money out of the Doves, and that would be no insuperable difficulty. If the Doves are determined to quit the country, as you suppose, they will, I feel certain, not be stopped for the sake of a few hundred pounds. They must be very wealthy now that they have obtained my aunt's fortune."

"True," responded Mr. Agile, "but you see there are only five minutes allowed at Dover between the arrival of the train and the departure of the steamer, and therefore a slight interference will be sufficient to cause them to miss the boat. However, if we catch the train at Cannon Street, we shall have them safely enough without the need of any interference on the part of others."

"Drive faster," he called out to the cabman, and the horses were hurried on as fast as the crowded thorough-fare would permit, but all to no purpose.

Mr. Agile had attempted an impossibility. With a clear road, and permission to go at full gallop, he might have succeeded, but with constant interruptions in the traffic, and the prohibition which stood in the way of furious driving, such a result was quite out of the question.

Mr. Agile would have seen this had he been less
flurried, but his nerves, and indeed those of the whole
party, were so strained by the intense excitement of the
chase, that the commission of a slight error in judgment
is not to be wondered at.

"We cannot do anything now but wait for the next
train, which does not go until to-morrow morning," said
Mr. Agile, looking annoyed at having arrived at the
station too late; and after saying this, he advised that
the party should separate for the night, and meet in
the station at an early hour on the following morning—
the Detectives having first undertaken to communicate
without delay with the police at Dover by telegram.

Frank utilized the evening by settling his account with
the auctioneer, arranging for the forwarding of the furniture, and in writing to his father and Mr. Jeffries. He
would have been glad if his friendship with May had
been such as would have permitted him to correspond
with her, but he felt that to do so would be to presume
upon their short acquaintance, and perhaps hinder his
cause. However, he did not fail to send her a message
in the note he addressed to his father, which, if she
cared at all for him, she could not fail to appreciate.

"As soon as this business is settled," he said to himself, "I will not lose any time in getting to her side,

and in making a declaration of my passion. My present condition is so unsettled—every breeze that blows seems to so move and affect me, that I am afraid of the consequences which might ensue from any lengthy delay. There are some men who feel no longing for the society and influence of a lovely, charming woman—who exhibit no interest in any existence but their own, and perhaps that of some quadruped; whilst there are others who, on the contrary, can have no existence apart from that being which, from a human point of view, must be to man the ideal of creation. I am afraid I come under the second category," thought Frank, "but," he added, half aloud, in a serio-comic manner, "what sayeth the Poet on the subject of a wife?

'His house she enters there to be its light,
'Shining within when all around is night,
'Doubling his pleasures and his cares dividing,
'A guardian angel o'er his life presiding.'

"I feel quite poetical this evening," he continued, "I fancy love and poetry go hand in hand. How I love that darling girl! Her movements are so graceful, her voice so musical, her manner so winning—would that I could call her by the endearing term of wife!— it would simply be 'supreme'"—and here Frank gave a long, low whistle, which conveyed more clearly than any words could the overwhelming and rapturous nature of the feelings which filled his heart.

> "'New ways I must attempt my grov'ling name
> To raise aloft, and wing my flight to fame.'"

said Frank, continuing his meditations. "What a great incentive to action love is! I feel to-night that I could dare and do anything, even to the making of the greatest sacrifice, to win May's approbation and to give her pleasure. It must be, as Virgil says:

> 'In hell and earth and seas and heaven above,
> Love conquers all, and we must yield to love.'"

CHAPTER XI.

THE morning came, and at the appointed time our friends met at the station.

"Has anything been heard from the police at Dover?" Mr. Agile asked, after first exchanging the usual civilities.

"We had a telegram late last night," replied one of the detectives, "but they say they have not seen anyone at Dover answering the description we gave, and they are positive in asserting that no such personage crossed to Calais in last night's steamer."

"We surely cannot be on the wrong track," said Mr. Agile, musingly. "Even the information gleaned from the auctioneer would point to the fact that Mr. Dove has left for the Continent, and he would certainly go *via* Dover. At all events we will go on to Dover. I have a sort of feeling that we shall be in time, and will succeed in arresting our man. Come, here is the train now."

The party entered, and were soon being rapidly borne along to their destination—rapidly the avenger of wrongs, by human agency, was tracking the wicked ones in their flight, and would soon overtake and wreak upon them the punishment they had so richly merited.

Justice ever stands with unsheathed sword and uplifted hand; and though the stroke may seem to be delayed in its delivery, it will most certainly descend upon the heads of the guilty ones with crushing force and power.

Mr. Dove and his son, as also Jerry and Will Mills, had, though unknown to the police, reached Dover on the previous evening, in time for the boat, but Mr. Dove felt so unwell on arriving, that Charles deemed it would be imprudent to cross the Channel that night, and he and his father had therefore proceeded to an hotel, intending to resume their journey on the morrow.

Jerry and his son, after following their late employers to the hotel, took up their quarters in one of more modest pretensions.

Here they talked over their affairs, and resolved in the morning to pay the Doves a visit in person, make known their object, and extract at all hazards a good round sum from them.

Jerry had armed himself with a revolver, so that it was clearly evident that he intended to press his claims by means of what he considered the strongest of all arguments,—brute force.

Picture the surprise of the Doves, at breakfast, on the following day, when, after quietly congratulating themselves upon their escape, and talking of the brighter days before them, the waiter announced that two persons named Mills wished to see them immediately.

"We know no one of that name, and further, we cannot be troubled with any visits this morning," said Mr. Dove, and the attendant quitted the apartment with his message.

"I thought we were clear of those scoundrels," said Mr. Dove, turning to Charles. "What shall we do now? I am afraid of that Mills; he has been a source of great anxiety to me lately, and has been so threatening in his manner that I fear he contemplates doing us some bodily harm."

"If he wants money let him have some," said Charles, "and then we shall be rid of him."

"That is all very well. We want the money ourselves. And then the more the fellow gets the more he wants," replied Mr. Dove.

"The way of the world," rejoined Charles, shrugging his shoulders.

At this stage in the conversation the waiter again entered, this time bringing with him a note, and stating that the men were still in attendance, and would not listen to the answer which Mr. Dove had sent.

Snatching the note up petulantly, Mr. Dove tore it open, and Charles, who was looking over his shoulder, read as follows :—

"Dear Sirs,

"The knowledge of your intention to quit England "having come unexpectedly into my possession, I have "thought that you would probably like, before finally "leaving, to favour me with some more cash in con- "sideration of the valuable service I rendered you *in* "*obtaining Mrs. Walton's fortune.*

"I should much regret being forced to resort to the "various means at my disposal of compelling you to "meet my demands, and trust, therefore, you will not "give me occasion to do so.

"My son, who pens this note, and who, although he "did not in any way participate in the carrying out of "your instructions, is fully cognizant of all the details, "*including those respecting certain Manchester business,*

"will, if we are not immediately met in this matter,
"take such action as will place you where money will
"no longer serve your ends.

"Awaiting your decision,

"I am,

"Yours most humbly,

"JERRY MILLS.

"Per W. M."

"Waiter, leave the room for a moment," said Mr.
Dove; and as soon as he and Charles were alone, he
continued—"How could this fellow become acquainted
with anything respecting Mrs. Walton and Manchester
business? This is most unfortunate, and now that that
fellow Atherton is abroad, our position becomes one of
greater danger each moment we delay. I am afraid we
must yield to this fellow's demands, or we shall be
stopped. He evidently contemplates mischief. What do
you think about it, Charles?"

Give him two or three hundred pounds; tell him he
is mistaken about our leaving England for good; that
we shall be back in a fortnight, and that we shall then
perhaps be in a position to let him have some more
cash. Once we reach the Continent we shall be free.
Better send for and get rid of them at once," said
Charles.

"Good," responded Mr. Dove. "Waiter, show those men up."

Jerry and his son entered, and as the sun shone through the window upon them, the former looked in the clear light to be a perfect demon. He was irritated at the manner in which he had been kept waiting, and his passion seemed to fairly flash out of his eyes. Jerry had never been good looking, but since his nose had been broken by the blow Frank had dealt him, and his face had been otherwise disfigured, his appearance was perfectly repulsive.

Mr. Dove and even Charles quaked when they looked at him, and it was but with difficulty and in a trembling voice that Mr. Dove could ask him what he wanted.

"Nowt less than a thousand pounds this time," replied Jerry.

"Tut, tut, impossible, man; where should I get a thousand pounds from to give you now? You know you deceived me in the matter of young Atherton."

Jerry rather staggered at this last remark, but assuming a dogged air he replied:

"I don't care where yer gets the coin from; all as I says is I must have it quick. Young Atherton won't trouble you any more, that I knows.

J

"I saw Atherton in London yesterday with my own eyes, apparently as well as ever."

"You're a liar!" said Jerry, yer might have seen somebody like him, but not him, that I'm certain on. Now out with the cash!" he said, fumbling in the pocket in which he had placed his revolver, at the same time, however, remembering with horror the vision he had had in London.

"Well, I will give you a couple of hundred pounds for the sake of peace," said Mr. Dove, "and, probably, as I am only going away for a short time, another couple on my return."

"Won't take nothin' less than a thou'," said Jerry.

"Give him a cheque for the amount he asks," said Charles to his father, "and close this unpleasant interview—your health will not permit of this excitement."

Mr. Dove took the hint, knowing that his banking account had been almost closed before he left Manchester, and producing his cheque book, he was about to write out a cheque for the amount, when Jerry stopped him.

"None o' that paper for me—hard cash—come, part, or I'll send you to ——."

He did not say where, but he produced his revolver and pointed it at Mr. Dove, who, on seeing the weapon, dropped behind the table in a fright.

"Take the money—take the money," he gasped. "Charles, give it to .him and let him go."

Charles, in as great a terror as his father, obeyed the latter's instruction with alacrity, being only too glad to get rid of Jerry on any terms.

After the money was paid over, Jerry said, with a leer, as he and his son quitted the room : "Mornin' gents. No thanks to yer—yer owes yer thanks to me for not makin' yer part with more coin."

On reaching the street they proceeded to the railway station, with the view of returning to London, little dreaming as they did so that they were walking right into the hands of the detectives, who were accompanying Frank and Mr. Agile in the rapidly-approaching train.

Mr. Agile, who was sitting close to the window, noticed young Mills as the train drew up at the platform. "There," said he, jumping up and turning to Frank, "is the young sailor fellow I told you about, and in company with a man answering the description of the one you struck so heavily."

"It is he," said Frank, looking in the direction indicated by his solicitor. "Quick ! secure them."

The detectives sprang out and pounced upon Jerry and his companion before they had time to realise the intention of their opponents.

Jerry, although he struggled hard to shake off the two men who had seized him, was soon handcuffed and quite at their mercy. Not so, however, was the the case with young Mills. When he felt the detectives grasp him, instead of standing up to combat with them, he sank to the platform; and before they had the slightest inkling of his intentions, he had thrown them both to the ground, slipped out of the garments which had been grasped, jumped between the carriages of the train, passed to the opposite side of the line, and disappeared from sight almost before the surprised group of people which had gathered in the station could learn what had happened.

Although search was subsequently made, nothing was ever discovered as to the whereabouts of young Mills, but let us hope that, on learning the penalty which his father had to pay for the crimes which he had committed, he saw the error of the course he had followed, and amended his ways.

Mr. Agile and Frank, knowing that the time within which they had to make the further arrest was short, if, indeed, Mr. Dove and his son had not escaped them, waited only to see Jerry secured, and then, with three policemen who had come to meet them at Dover, they rushed off to the packet, which was waiting at the pier. Here the men were making ready to let go the steamer, but Frank, gliding up to the captain, explained the case in a few words, and obtained a brief delay.

Mr. Agile, in the meantime, had descended to the cabin with his men.

" Here they are," he said, pointing out Mr. Dove and Charles, who were seated at a table talking.

The men advanced, and as they did so Mr. Dove, happening to look up, caught sight of their uniform and threatening appearance. With a cry he fell backwards in a swoon, and Charles, springing to his feet, saw at a glance that it was useless for him to offer any resistance. He, therefore, allowed the police to arrest him, and to lead him forth. Mr. Dove was carried on to the quay, and the vessel's moorings being loosened, she glided away from her berth rapidly towards the sea.

The prisoners were conveyed to Chester, and there lodged in gaol to await their trial.

In the interim Mr. Agile occupied himself in working up Frank's case, and succeeded in securing for him at least two-thirds of the fortune left by Mrs. Walton, the £1,000 which Jerry had obtained a short time previously to his capture being included in that sum.

The detectives had searched Jerry's home in Liverpool, and had there found documents which, if Jerry had not made a confession, would have been sufficient to

When the trial came on, however, Jerry seeing that his case was hopeless, divulged all the facts implicating the Doves, taking care to place his own performances in the best light possible. The men who had been his accomplices, he explained, were drowned on the eventful night upon which the attack was made upon Frank, concluding his declaration by stating that his son was entirely innocent in the matter.

Then he appealed for mercy, on the ground that this was his first offence (he having previously evaded detection), and that he was tempted from the paths of virtue by the promise made to him, by the other prisoners, of a large sum of money, and the ease which he thought that money would bring with it. He hoped, he further said, that his years would also be taken as a reason why his sentence should be made as light as possible.

The Doves, under the advice of their solicitor, also pleaded guilty, and threw themselves upon the mercy of the Court.

It remained, therefore, only for the sentence to be pronounced, and this the Judge did in a very impressive manner.

Mr. Dove and his son, being the chief offenders, were sentenced to twenty and Jerry Mills to fifteen

The Judge, in summing up, pointed out the serious nature of the offences which had been committed, dwelt for some time upon the wisdom of honouring and abiding by the law, and concluded by hoping that the decision which they had that day arrived at would go forth to the country as a warning to all such desperadoes and villains as those upon whom sentence had just been passed.

After the conclusion of the case Frank bade adieu to his solicitor, and quitted the city for home.

Frank's father had, it must be remarked, now quite recovered in health, and had resumed his ordinary business occupation in Liverpool. He was, we may be certain, glad to get his boy back again, healthy and strong, after all the anxiety he had suffered on his account.

"Frank, my boy," he said, after they had spent a couple of hours together, "you must go to Crompton to-morrow and pay a visit to Mr. and Miss Jeffries. They will be glad to see you, and I feel we owe them both a deep debt of gratitude."

"Certainly," replied Frank, "with all my heart. It was my intention to do so."

And the morrow found him at Crompton, with what result we shall shortly learn.

CHAPTER XII.

THE train sped on rapidly from Liverpool to Crompton, but to Frank it seemed that it had never travelled so slowly.

However, he eventually arrived, and a short time afterwards he was comfortably ensconced in Squire Jeffries' drawing-room, relating to his eager listeners the story of his adventures.

He noticed, with inward satisfaction, the blush which momentarily suffused May's face as he entered her home; and it soon became evident to him, although she made an effort to conceal the state of her feelings, that she regarded him with more than common interest.

And what was Frank's experience, now that he again found himself in May's presence? Did he feel perfectly at his ease in this his longed-for interview?

In confidence we reply that Frank's feelings were

those which a true and faithful love ever generates,—
a fluttering at the heart, a heightened colour, a slight
hesitation in speech—these were amongst the character-
istics of his warm, genuine affection, which made themselves unpleasantly recognisable to our hero.

It is, we think, a sign that there exists in the
heart of the man ˙who is perfectly *sang froid* and glib
of tongue in an ordeal of the kind through which Frank
was passing, but very little love, if indeed it can be
granted that any refining sentiment holds a place there.

True it is, that so engrossing was Frank's love for
May, that, when left alone with her, he felt quite unable
to keep up a conversation on ordinary topics. So it
happened that, when the Squire good-naturedly left them
tête-a-tête, instead of utilizing the moments by making a
declaration and a proposal, Frank lapsed into silence
—a silence which May made no effort to disturb, and
which was broken only by the ticking of the old-fashioned
clock which occupied a corner in the room.

How May had longed for this time to come! And
now that it had arrived, she required no words to com·
plete her happiness. She had seen that Frank reciprocated her love; and this silence not only confirmed
the fact, but left her mind, as it did Frank's, free to
enjoy the bright visions which seemed to pervade the

very atmosphere they breathed, and to fill them with a secret pleasure.

"Frank," said the Squire, on re-entering the room after a short absence, "you must make yourself cosy here for at least a fortnight. You have had so much excitement and worry of late, that rest is imperative. Besides, both May and myself can do with a little company, and, therefore, I do not intend to take any refusal. I told your father that I should keep you here for a week or two when you paid me a visit, so that you may make your mind easy on that score."

"Oh, yes, of course Mr. Atherton will stay," said May, looking rather wistfully at Frank.

If Frank had had any intention of refusing the Squire's kind invitation, May's addendum certainly put it to flight, and he answered:

"Thank you, Squire; I feel that I can do with a slight rest before I resume my business occupations, and, therefore, I will gladly avail myself of your kindness."

On parting for the night, Frank could not resist pressing May's hand a little warmly; and as the pressure was recognised and returned, he retired with a heart almost bursting with gladness.

The following morning he rose early, and with a

light, joyful heart. The morning was a splendid one, and as Frank gazed from the window, he could not help saying:—"My sorrow seems to have passed away like glistening dewdrops do beneath the radient sunshine. Ah! I have now the longed-for inspiration! We will pen the antithesis."

Taking up a sheet of paper, he wrote:—

"The rosy light of morn has sped
  Its shafts like tender spray,
And chased from out their wonted bed,
  The steeds of night away:
And warbling music comes and goes,
  Like breath of sweetest flow'rs,
And nature all her beauty shews
  In these her fairest hours.

" Then memory dissolve the past,
  With all its gloom and pain,
And ne'er by clouds be overcast,
  But present joys retain !!
And memory attends the cry,
  And with compassion moves
The burden of my former sigh,
  My haunting dream disproves."

"I am glad that is off my mind," he said on rising. "After all it is a relief to write a little poetry sometimes. It has been said that for a man to write poetry is to display a sign of weakness, unless, indeed, he is possessed of genius; but really I feel, with all due respect to the author of the remark, that to write even a few poor verses at times is a great relief to my oppressed nature."

Mental joys are, in some degree, burdensome, in that we feel we like to share them with others, and we know of no safer and more pleasurable outlet for them than the reducing of them to written verse.

It needed but a few days to sweep away the barrier of reserve which delicacy had erected between Frank and May, and to place the young people on terms of the most intimate friendship.

The formalities of "Mr." and "Miss" were, of course, soon dispensed with; and the felicity of a few quiet rambles in the charming rural districts which surrounded Crompton, sufficed to give them that freedom and openness in their communications with one another which are almost invariably the result of lovers' walks in country lanes.

One morning, when they were thus passing the time, Frank felt he must know his fate. Gently slipping his arm through May's for the first time, he again lapsed into silence.

May intuitively knew that something important would succeed the calm this time, and she judged rightly. It was, however, broken in an unexpected manner.

"May," he said, drawing her more closely to him, whilst she held her breath, "I shall never be happy until I know that I may call you mine!!"

She blushed deeply but answered not, whilst he proceeded :—

"May, I cannot, dare not, think of life without you, my darling——."

"Oh, Frank," said May, looking very bashfully at him, "how can you say——?"

"But," he interrupted, "you will be my own darling wife, will you not?"

Her drooping eyelids and her whole manner so clearly betokened her consent, that without waiting for a verbal answer he had placed his arm around her, and——but we will draw the curtain over this most tender scene. Frank only did what lovers usually do, and therefore we must leave it to the imagination of each reader to picture to his or her taste the various little incidents which fill up the happy days of courtship.

We must, however, not refrain from recounting one little occurrence which ever afterwards formed one of those pleasing episodes around which memory clusters with fondness.

One morning, after his engagement had been made known to and approved of by the Squire, Frank was alone in the garden, thinking he was a very happy fellow, and how he could best amuse and please May. "Well," he said, "I must, I suppose, invoke the Muses as usual."

Extracting a leaf from his pocket-book, he sat down on an adjacent seat, and was soon busily engaged with his self-imposed task.

Whilst he was thus occupied, May, who had come into the garden to keep him company, observed his attitude, and guessing what he was about, she gently stole towards him on tip-toe.

Busily Frank wrote, and May peeping over his shoulder, read :—

> "I often think of thee, my love,
>   At cheerful dawn of day,
> When all is clear and happy love,
>   And sorrow far away.
> Methinks the smiling morn, my May,
>   Reflects thy joyous face,
> Whilst gladsome sunbeams sportive play
>   Around thee to embrace.
>
> "Thy form is seen in all that's fair,
>   Symmetrical, sublime,
> And bears an impress and an air
>   Of some far better clime:
> Thy laugh resembles most the rill
>   Which winds through glen and glade,
> And sweetly rippling stirs the still,
>   And variegates the shade.

"Then wonder not, my darling May,
　Why I thy charms admire,
And why thy vision day by day,
　My deeds and thoughts inspire;
Or most of all why I so oft,
　(Ah think it not amiss),
Desire to press thy lips so soft,
　In one sweet ling'ring ———."

Frank never finished the rhyme, at least not on paper, for at the moment he was about to write the word, he felt his ear being pulled, and heard a charming voice saying: "You naughty boy, writing such rubbish." "Take that," she said, giving his ear another pull, and then bounded away with the ease and grace of a fawn. Frank dropped the paper and made chase, and ere long had concluded his poem by means of a rhyming action, which produced a sensation sweeter than any word ever coined could do.

Frank of course wanted, as our American cousins say, to get married "right away," but the Squire would not agree to this. "No," he said, "I cannot spare May until after Christmas. We must have a merry time together first, and then, if the Lord wills it, early in January you may take my darling from me."

Poor old man, he almost cried as he said this. He had been so happy with his daughter, so very,

very happy. She had been so loving and obedient, so kind and cheerful in her manner, that to part with her the Squire felt was to deprive himself of all that afforded him temporal pleasure.

"But," he would say inwardly, "it is God's will, and why should I place myself between her and Frank, whom I know she loves dearly? God bless you both," he added aloud, "and depend upon it that if you trust your ways to Him He will make you happy and bless you in your new relationship. My experience is that of the Psalmist when he said: 'I have been young and now am old, yet have I not seen the righteous forsaken.'"

May threw herself upon her father's breast, and comforted the old man as only a daughter can. They would not leave him for long, and when they returned, oh, how they would love him, and make his days brighter and happier than ever they had been in the past.

Christmas was a long time coming, so at least thought Frank; but it did come at last, and round the Squire's hospitable board were again gathered a number of his friends, this time, however, including Frank and his father.

May and Frank "somehow" got together in a quiet corner, and May then told him all that had occurred

on the previous Christmas, how his absence and her
anxiety had revealed to her the love she entertained
for him. She also told him of her dream and subsequent hopes and misgivings, until Frank, under the
influence of her confidence and charms, could not but
think he had secured for a partner that inestimable
treasure, a true and loving woman.

"Confidence for confidence," said Frank. "May, darling, I have secured a charming villa in the suburbs of
Liverpool—in the words of the poet :

> 'A country cottage near a crystal flood,
> A winding valley and a lofty wood.'

I have had sent there some antique furniture which
formerly belonged to my aunt, and which I fortunately
secured at a sale in London."

"Ah, yes; I remember you said that you found your
aunt's Will in her cabinet, in London, but you never
told us how the cabinet came into your possession,"
said May.

"I had a reason for not doing so," replied Frank.
"Now there is no further cause to remain silent. What
would you have thought if I, a single young man, told
you I had purchased a quantity of furniture ?"

"Only that you contemplated housekeeping," laughed
May.

K

"Further," said Frank, "and this you will be pleased with, I have seen Betsy, to whom my aunt left an annuity, and she has expressed a desire to occupy the same position in *our* house as that which she filled so ably in my aunt's."

"He's a good, kind, thoughtful boy," said May, gently caressing him, "and we shall see if we can make him happy bye and bye!"

"There is another thing, May, which I have omitted to mention, and that is the name we shall give to *our* house!"

"Yes; what shall it be?" said May, quite eagerly.

"You will remember that I told you about Captain Winkelstein," said Frank, "Well, he made me a suggestion on the subject which, if you are agreeable, we will adopt in remembrance of him."

And then Frank told her all that the kind-hearted captain had said; and May was so pleased with the recital that she must, of course, rush off to papa to share the joy with him.

The wedding morning came. Not a cloud darkened the horizon, and the bells of the Old Church rang out a merry peal. Weddings at Crompton were not every day occurrences, and on such occasions the inhabitants for the greater part considered it their duty to witness the ceremony.

May being a general favourite, there was a larger
gathering at the church to witness her wedding than
had previously been known, and the pathway leading
to the door of the sacred edifice was lined with bright
rosy-cheeked girls, who, as the happy couple passed
along, strewed flowers before them, to the tune of an
old wedding song, which told of rosy pathways in an
unclouded future.

There remains now but little to recount.

Frank, on returning from his honeymoon, which he
spent in the south of France, took up his abode at
"Mayville," where one morning he had a glad surprise
in the shape of a visit from Captain Winkelstein.

"Potztausend," said that worthy, as he met Frank
in the garden, "joost vat I said vood be zee case.
'Mayville' on zee garden gate, und I'll vet von trifle
May mit in (within) zee castle."

"You are right, captain," said Frank, "and I am
very glad to see the author of the name. Come
into the castle; I will introduce you to it's queen."

"Goot," said the captain laughingly, "you have not
forgotten zee story."

"No, and not likely to do so," said Frank.

After a long chat on all that had occurred on Frank's
memorable voyage, the captain said, rather slyly :—

"You know, Master Frank, dis courtin' bisnis is sehr (very) infectious, I tink you calls him, und, after hearing you talk so much, I felt dat, perhaps, it vood be vell mit zee captain if he had zee prospect of von fine voman for von vife."

"Good," said Frank, "and have you made any progress in that direction, captain?"

"I tinks so," replied the captain, "seeing dat I am to be married in von veek fon now, mit von of zee most bevitching darlings in creation, und dat I am come to ask you to be at zee vedding."

"With all my heart," rejoined Frank.

And here, on the threshold of a future bright with promise, we think we had better bid adieu to Frank and May and their friends; and as we shake hands with them, let us wish that all their fond hopes may end in joyful fulfilment, and that finally they may enter into the possession of that better inheritance which God has set apart for those who love him!

THE LIVERPOOL PRINTING AND STATIONERY COMPANY, LIMITED 38, CASTLE STREET.

CPSIA information can be obtained at www.ICGtesting.com
Printed in the USA
LVOW081438180613

339153LV00004B/96/P